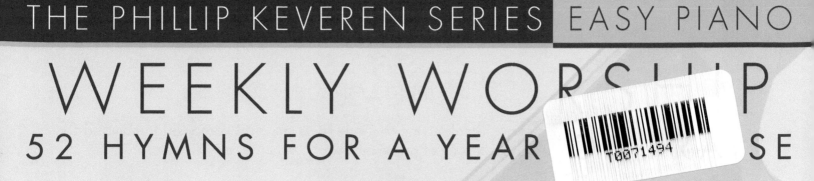

WEEKLY WORSHIP
52 HYMNS FOR A YEAR OF PRAISE

— PIANO LEVEL —
Intermediate

ISBN 978-1-4950-1921-0

HAL•LEONARD® CORPORATION

7777 W. BLUEMOUND RD. P.O. BOX 13819 MILWAUKEE, WI 53213

Visit Hal Leonard Online at
www.halleonard.com

Visit Phillip at
www.phillipkeveren.com

PREFACE

Hymn: 1a. A song of praise or thanksgiving to God; 1b. A metrical composition adapted for singing in a religious service; 2. A song of praise or joy.

There are hundreds of hymns that could have appeared in this collection. So, the challenge was to narrow the list down to 52, and we set out in pursuit of that objective. One can find numerous Top 100, Top 50, Top 25 compilations in myriad formats – from books to recordings to sheet music. My suspicion is that all of these lists of favorites, like *Weekly Worship*, were influenced by the life experiences of the person(s) putting them together. My mother's favorite hymn, "What a Friend We Have in Jesus," simply had to be in this book. "Joyful, Joyful, We Adore Thee," in my opinion, stands as one of the finest hymns ever penned. It is, quite possibly, my favorite hymn. It somehow made its way into this book!

If you are a young developing pianist, my hope is that you will improve your musical skills through the study of these arrangements. More importantly, my prayer is that you will deepen your understanding of God's truths that are at the heart of these timeless expressions of faith.

If you are an adult musician, one who sang these hymns over many decades, I hope this book will bring back precious memories from your journey.

On a personal note: I asked my daughter, Lindsay, to write the "hymn history" segments that appear with each song. Her academic preparation, writing talent, and heart for Christ and His church made her a natural collaborator on this project. It was a joy to work with her, one that I will always treasure.

–Phillip Keveren

BIOGRAPHY

Phillip Keveren, a multi-talented keyboard artist and composer, has composed original works in a variety of genres from piano solo to symphonic orchestra. Mr. Keveren gives frequent concerts and workshops for teachers and their students in the United States, Canada, Europe, and Asia. Mr. Keveren holds a B.M. in composition from California State University Northridge and a M.M. in composition from the University of Southern California.

Growing up in a home where music of nearly every style was being played or composed each day, it took a lot for me to really "hate" a piece of music. Because Phillip Keveren is my father, I learned to appreciate the artistry of pretty much every genre of music, unless it was overtly distasteful or dishonoring to God. However, there is one type of music I did not always understand or exactly "like" when I was growing up. You guessed it; I'm talking about church hymns.

The churches my family attended in my growing up years kept a steady balance between the use of contemporary praise songs and traditional hymns. Unfortunately, when we sang hymns, I impatiently counted the lines that still remained to be sung. I truly could not wait to get to what I saw as a more upbeat, emotionally relevant contemporary worship song. When we sang hymns, it felt like we were singing archaic language and outdated melodies. However, I did notice that the elderly people in our congregation always seemed to get into the hymns in much the same way as I and other people my age got into the contemporary songs.

After I graduated from high school in 2006 and flew from the nest of my parents' home, I attended Asbury University. During my time at college, I learned to love God more deeply than I ever had in my life. I experienced a fresh outpouring of the Holy Spirit, and I began to see worship as something that should encompass my entire life, not just the limited time when worship music is played at chapel or at church. I even began to enjoy hymns, because I began to appreciate the rich Scriptural references that are present in many of them. In May 2010, I graduated with a liberal arts degree in Bible-Theology. Now I am working on a Master of Divinity at Asbury Theological Seminary, and my appreciation for Holy Scripture, church history, and Christian tradition has only grown stronger.

These days, when I read and sing the historical hymns of the church, I realize I am not alone in my desire to know and worship God with all that I am. When I read the stories that inspired these hymns, I realize that the men and women who wrote them are a part of the "cloud of witnesses" that cheer each Christian on to know the heights and depths of Love Himself (Eph. 3:17-19). One day all of the redeemed will all sing a new song together, as we gather in the presence of our beautiful Savior (Rev. 15:2-4).

"Therefore, since we are surrounded by such a great cloud of witnesses, let us throw off everything that hinders and the sin that so easily entangles. And let us run with perseverance the race marked out for us, fixing our eyes on Jesus, the pioneer and perfecter of faith" (Hebrews 12:1-2a).

–Lindsay Rickard

BIOGRAPHY

Lindsay Rickard is a freelance writer. She graduated from Asbury University with a B.A. in Bible-Theology. In preparation for a life of teaching and discipleship ministry, she is currently pursuing an M. Div. at Asbury Theological Seminary. Lindsay and her husband, Nathan, reside in Wilmore, Kentucky.

CONTENTS

ABIDE WITH ME

Late in the summer of 1847, just months before his death, 54-year-old Henry Francis Lyte penned the words of this timeless hymn. Heavy-laden with tuberculosis, Lyte knew his days on earth were drawing to a close. As a minister with deep faith, he did not fear what would come after death. Instead, Lyte's hymn speaks of his longing to know Christ's abiding presence in the midst of his painful sickness and in the uncertain experience of death he would soon face. He knew Christ had been with him through every high and low of life. Now, his last request was for Christ to be near to him in death and to carry him home to abide with God forever.

Words by HENRY F. LYTE
Music by WILLIAM H. MONK
Arranged by Phillip Keveren

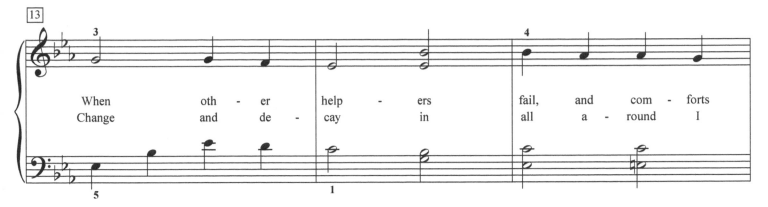

When oth - er help - ers fail, and com - forts
Change and de - cay in all a - round I

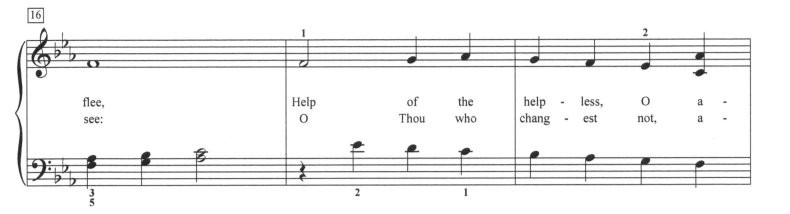

flee, Help of the help - less, O a -
see: O Thou who chang - est not, a -

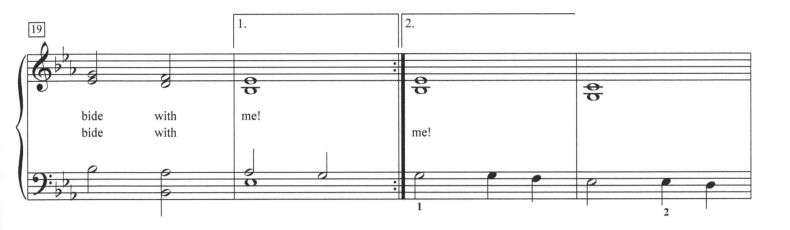

1.
bide with me!
bide with

2.
me!

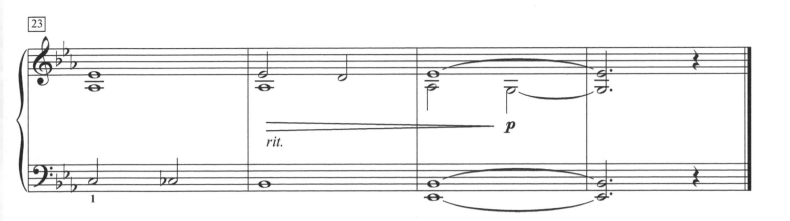

rit. _____ _p_

ALL CREATURES OF OUR GOD AND KING

St. Francis of Assisi, the Catholic Church's patron saint of animals, was born in Italy to a rich merchant in the late second century. By his early twenties, he had renounced all wealth and taken to the streets to actively demonstrate Christ's love to the poor, the lepers, and even the animals. He later founded the Franciscan order and helped to revitalize the Catholic Church of his day. His "Canticle of the Sun," later paraphrased into the English version "All Creatures of our God and King," is simply the summary of St. Francis's life purpose. He lived his life as a song of praise to his Creator and spent his life urging all of creation to join in the song.

Words by FRANCIS OF ASSISI
Translated by WILLIAM HENRY DRAPER
Music from *Geistliche Kirchengesang*
Arranged by Phillip Keveren

Stately (♩ = 80)

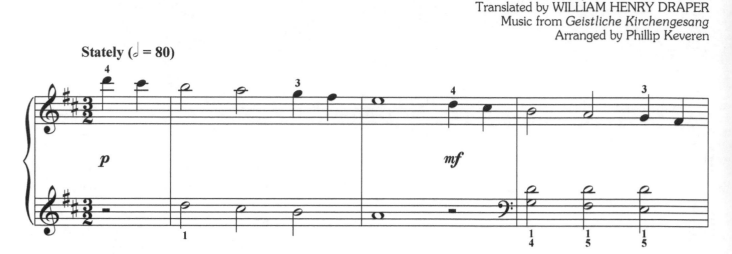

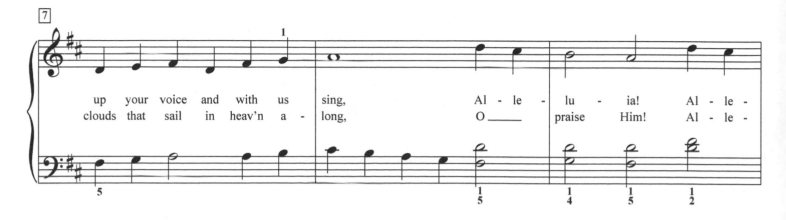

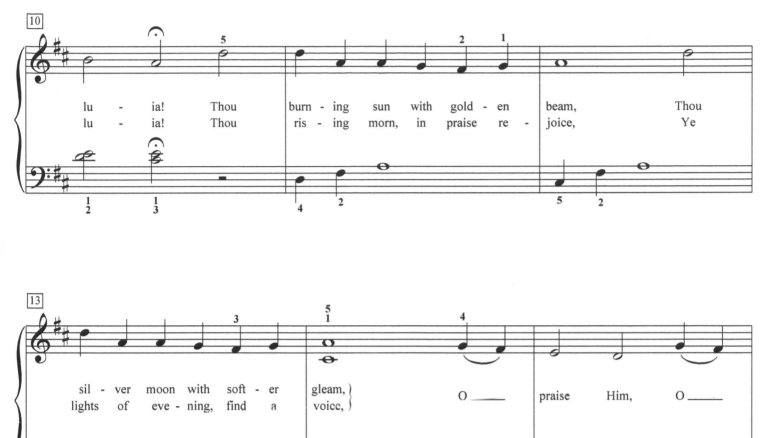

lu - ia! Thou burn - ing sun with gold - en beam, Thou
lu - ia! Thou ris - ing morn, in praise re - joice, Ye

sil - ver moon with soft - er gleam, ⎫
lights of eve - ning, find a voice, ⎭ O ____ praise Him, O ____

praise Him, Al - le - lu - ia! Al - le - lu - ia! A - le -

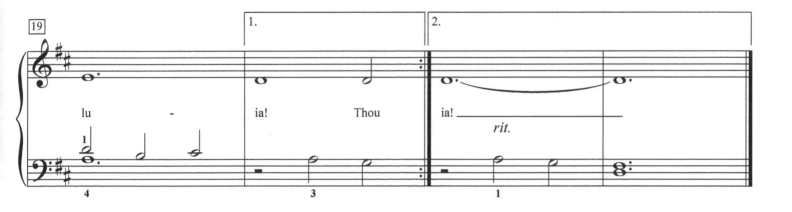

lu - ia! Thou ia! ____
rit.

ALL HAIL THE POWER OF JESUS' NAME

Edward Perronet, who lived in 18th-century England, is rumored to have been a passionate but temperamental minister who often preferred to argue over theological niceties than to seek humble unity with other Christians. It would seem that such a man could not be used by God to write this powerful hymn, but Edward is in good company in Scripture. Abraham had episodes of unbelief and fear, Moses was a murderer, Rahab was a prostitute, King David was an adulterer, St. Peter denied Christ in his darkest hour, and St. Paul martyred countless Christians. The power of Jesus' name is such that even utterly broken and sinful individuals like Edward and all of us can be transformed into vessels that bring honor and glory to our King.

Words by EDWARD PERRONET
Altered by JOHN RIPPON
Music by OLIVER HOLDEN
Arranged by Phillip Keveren

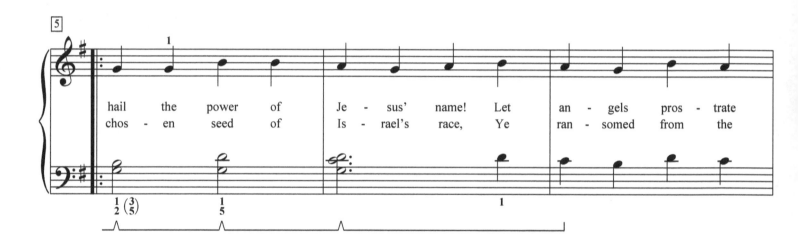

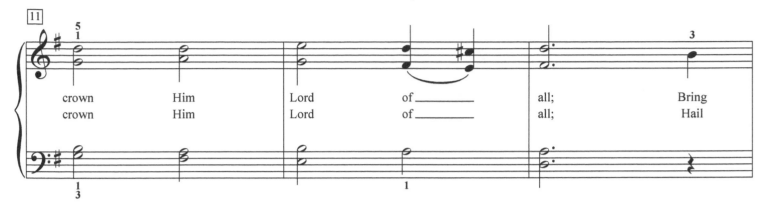

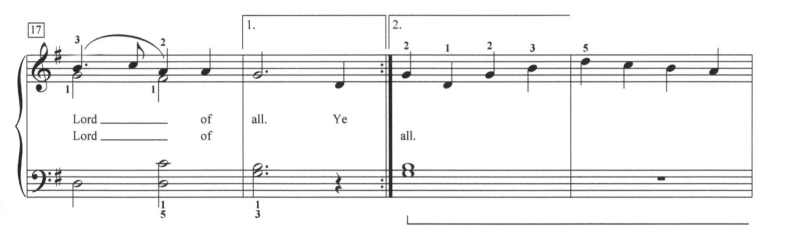

AMAZING GRACE

Once the cruel captain of a slave ship in the 18th century, John Newton abandoned the trade a few years after his conversion and actively supported William Wilberforce in his efforts to end the African slave trade in England. Knowing the full magnitude of his past sins, John Newton felt that God had saved him in order to demonstrate the glorious extent of his mercy and love. As a result, at age 40, Newton entered lifelong ministry. He eventually went blind, but this loss seems to have been of little consequence to Newton. He was forever healed of a far more terrible spiritual blindness that had long kept him from seeing and receiving the beautiful, amazing grace of God.

Words by JOHN NEWTON
From *A Collection of Sacred Ballads*
Traditional American Melody
From *Carrell and Clayton's Virginia Harmony*
Arranged by Phillip Keveren

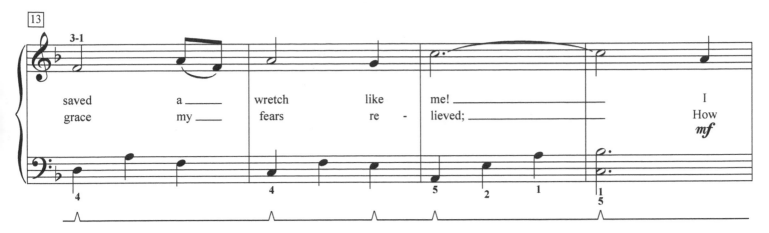

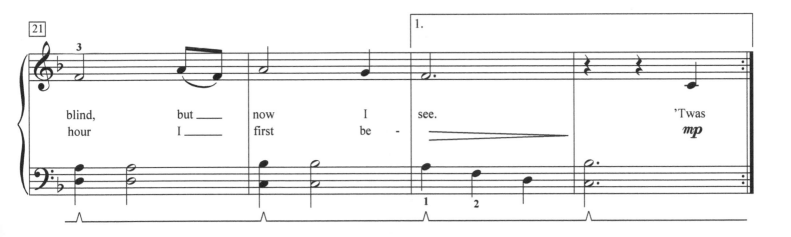

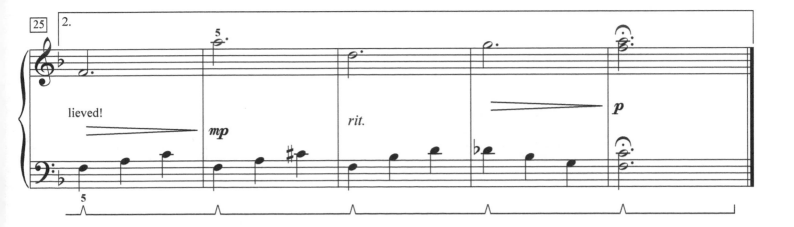

AND CAN IT BE
THAT I SHOULD GAIN

Charles Wesley had a conversion experience in 1738, but to an outside observer, he seemed the most zealous of Christians long before that. During his Oxford days, he helped his brother John start a club, dubbed the "Methodists" by onlookers, that was noted for its precise approach to the Christian life. Shortly after college, he became a missionary in Georgia, where he unsuccessfully sought to help others lead a serious Christian life. He returned to England discouraged, realizing that his legalistic religious exercises were missing something. Shortly after his conversion at a Moravian prayer meeting, Charles penned this hymn. In it, he wondered at the amazing love of Christ that is freely given, not earned by even the most sincere efforts of human beings.

Words by CHARLES WESLEY
Music by THOMAS CAMPBELL
Arranged by Phillip Keveren

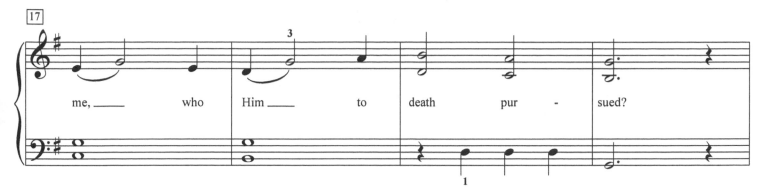

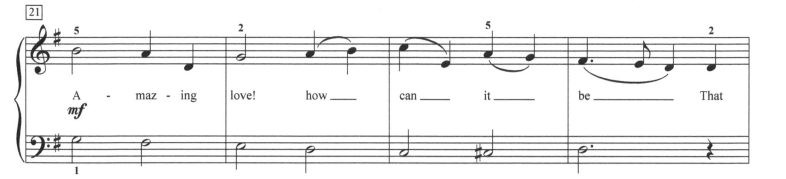

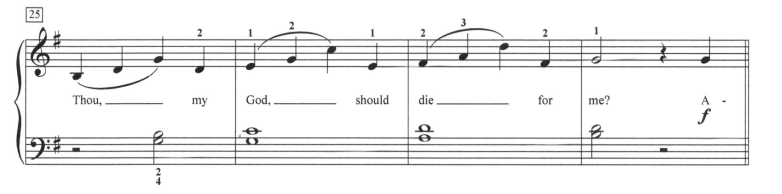

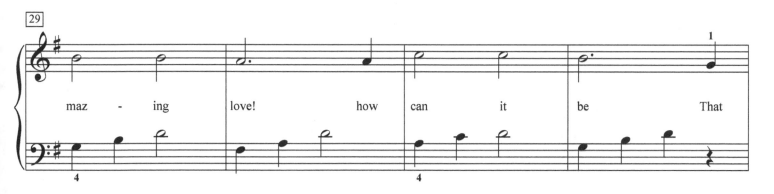

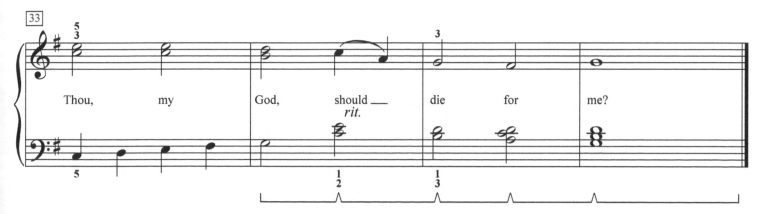

ANGELS WE HAVE HEARD ON HIGH

Over 2,000 years ago, ordinary and unsuspecting shepherds were watching over their flocks when a choir of angels filled the night sky. They announced the birth of Christ and then sang this refrain: "Glory to God in the highest and on earth peace, good will toward men" (Luke 2:14, KJV). The Christmas hymn we have today includes an anonymous French poem and a Latin version of the angels' song. "Gloria in excelsis Deo" means "Glory to God in the highest." This hymn resounds that angelic chorus, and their song becomes our anthem as we grasp the glorious reality of Christ's coming to earth on our behalf.

Traditional French Carol
Translated by JAMES CHADWICK
Arranged by Phillip Keveren

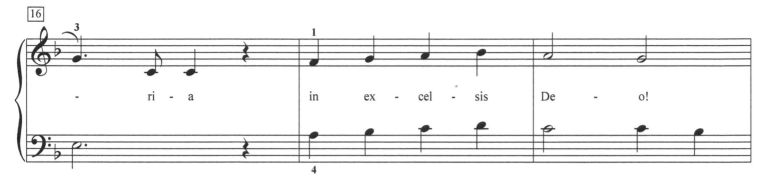

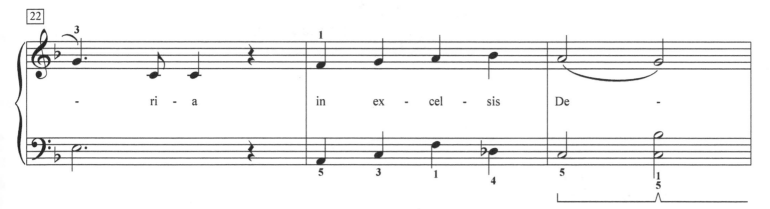

AT CALVARY

Those who have known the depths of their sin before coming to Christ often appreciate Jesus' work at Calvary more fully than most (Lk. 7:47). William Newell is no exception. As a wayward teen, his father pleaded with the president of Moody Bible Institute to admit his son into the college so he could perhaps find salvation. The president reluctantly agreed, under the condition that Newell would meet with him daily and do his best to follow the rules. William did find Christ at Moody, and, years later, he returned as a beloved Bible teacher. The lyrics of this hymn are the words of Newell's testimony: the story of how God pursued him as a prodigal and brought him home.

Words by WILLIAM R. NEWELL
Music by DANIEL B. TOWNER
Arranged by Phillip Keveren

Years I spent in van-i-ty and pride,
By God's Word at last my sin I learned;

Car-ing not my Lord was cru-ci-fied,
Then I trem-bled at the law I'd spurned,
Know-ing not it was for
Till my guilt-y soul im-

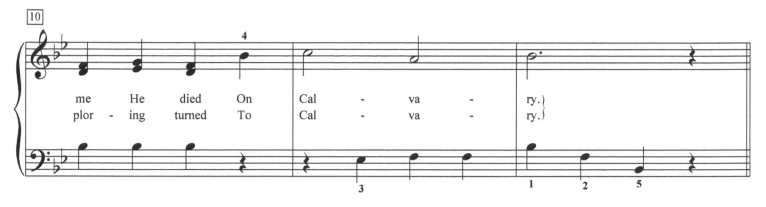

me He died On Cal - va - ry.)
plor - ing turned To Cal - va - ry.)

Mer - cy there was great, and grace was free; Par - don there was mul - ti -

plied to me; There my bur - dened soul found lib - er - ty, At

Cal - va - ry.

BE THOU MY VISION

In the fourth century A.D., a 16-year-old boy from Scotland was taken captive by pirates. This boy, Patrick, was enslaved in Ireland, and this is where he surrendered his life to Christ. He later escaped and returned to his home in Scotland, but God urged him to return to Ireland as a missionary at age 30. Thus began St. Patrick's fruitful ministry that yielded over 100,000 converts and around 200 church plants. Several centuries later, the thriving Irish churches were producing countless religious texts and songs. St. Dallan, an Irish poet during this period, wrote the lyrics of this hymn. St. Dallan may never have known Christ, let alone have penned this powerful prayer, were not God the all-consuming vision of St. Patrick's life and ministry.

Traditional Irish
Translated by MARY E. BYRNE
Arranged by Phillip Keveren

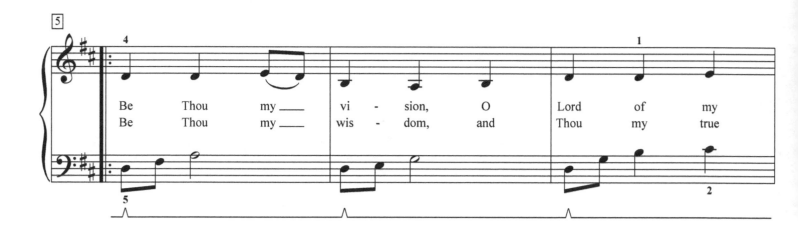

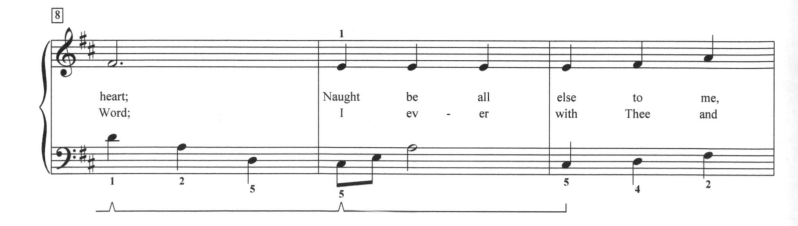

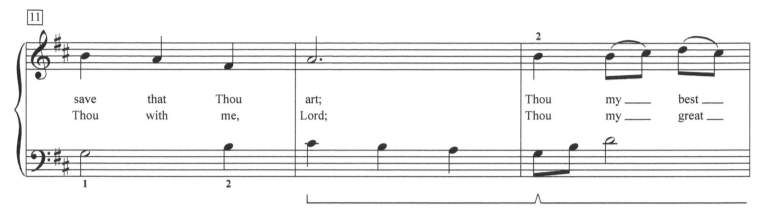

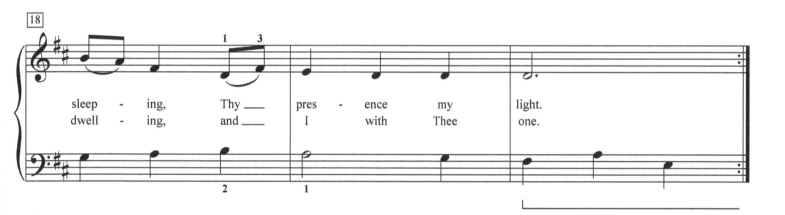

BLESSED ASSURANCE

From the time she was six weeks old, Fanny Crosby was blind, but this did not hinder her from writing over 8,000 hymn texts in her lifetime. At one point, Fanny was visiting her friend Phoebe Knapp, who often composed melodies and even wrote hymns of her own. Phoebe sat at the piano and played a tune, asking Fanny what the melody "said" to her. Fanny exclaimed, "That says, 'Blessed Assurance, Jesus is mine!'" Shortly thereafter, one of Fanny's most famous hymns was born. An equally famous hymnist from England, Ridley Havergal, once wrote a poem about her blind pen pal that included these perceptive lines: "Oh, her heart can see, her heart can see!/And its sight is strong and swift and free."

Lyrics by FANNY J. CROSBY
Music by PHOEBE PALMER KNAPP
Arranged by Phillip Keveren

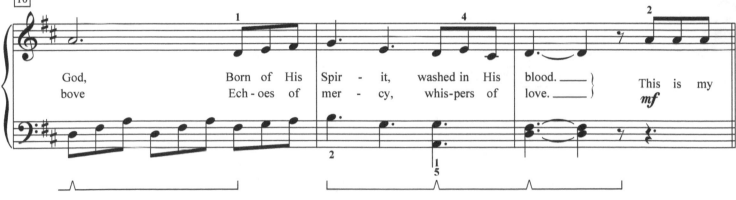

sto - ry, this is my song, Prais-ing my Sav - ior all the day

long; This is my sto - ry, this is my song, Prais-ing my

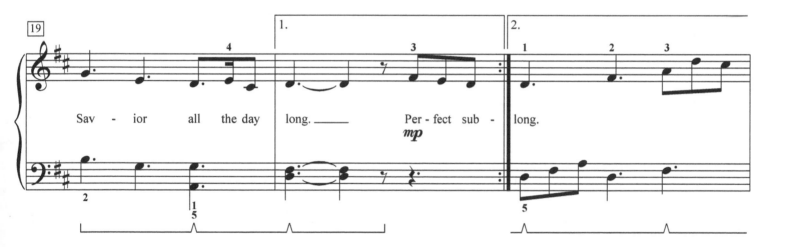

Sav - ior all the day long. _____ Per - fect sub - long.

mp

rit.   *p*

CHRIST THE LORD IS RISEN TODAY

Charles Wesley wrote the original version of this hymn around 1739. It had 11 stanzas, a different tune, and did not include
the "alleluias" of our modern-day version. During the 19th century, an anonymous person added the "alleluias" to the text
while he was trying to make it fit the tune we still use today. "Alleluia," short for "hallelujah" or "praise the Lord" in
Hebrew, is a fitting addition to a hymn that proclaims Christ's eternal victory over death. Though Christ's resurrection
is a historical event, this hymn speaks of it in the present tense. Christ the Lord is, not simply was,
risen and victorious over sin and death today, as He was 2,000 ago and will be forever. Praise the Lord!

Words by CHARLES WESLEY
Music adapted from *Lyra Davidica*
Arranged by Phillip Keveren

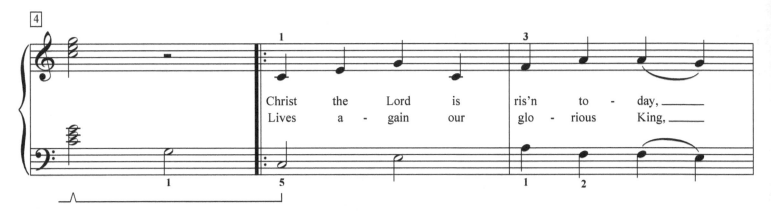

Christ the Lord is ris'n to - day, _____
Lives a - gain our glo - rious King, _____

Al - le - lu - ia! Sons of men and
Al - le - lu - ia! Where, O death, is

an - gels say: _____ Al - le - lu - ia!
now thy sting? _____ Al - le - lu - ia!

COME, THOU FOUNT OF EVERY BLESSING

Robert Robinson, a 23-year-old Baptist minister, wrote the lyrics of this hymn for use at his church on Pentecost Sunday, 1758. Appropriate to the occasion, the words are a prayer to the Holy Spirit, asking for help in singing God's praises and living the Christian life. Robinson himself knew the importance of the Holy Spirit's power in the life of a Christian. His teen years were wasted in debauchery and gang activity until he encountered Christ under the preaching of George Whitfield. It took three years for him to completely surrender his life to God, but when he did, he entered 30 years of fruitful, Spirit-empowered ministry. Robinson knew it was by the Spirit's power he was "rescue[d]… from danger" and would "safely… arrive at home."

Words by ROBERT ROBINSON
Music from John Wyeth's *Repository of Sacred Music*
Arranged by Phillip Keveren

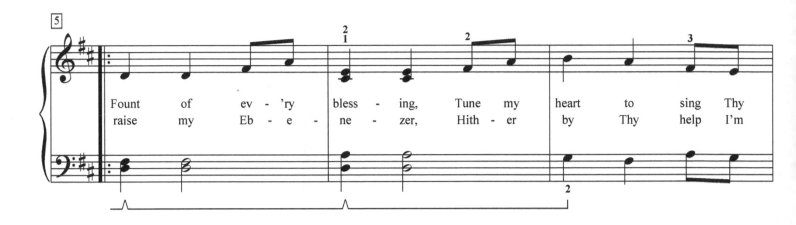

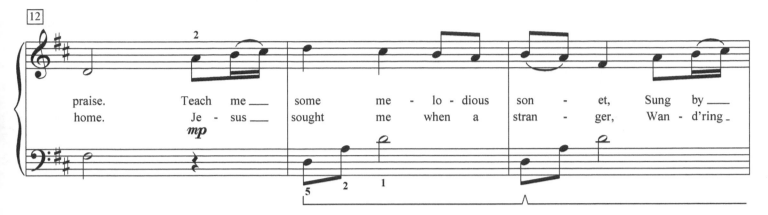

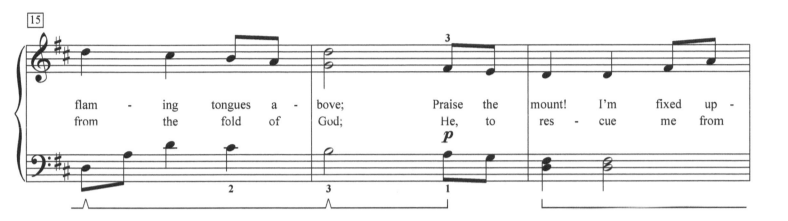

CROWN HIM WITH MANY CROWNS

Matthew Bridges, who had converted from Anglicanism to Catholicism, wrote the original six stanzas of this hymn text. He called it "The Song of the Seraphs," hearkening to the honor and worship of the Trinity that is happening 24/7 around the throne of God, as Revelation records. Years later, an Anglican clergyman named Godfrey Thring was concerned that Bridges' original version was exposing Protestants to controversial Catholic doctrine. He wrote six new stanzas for Protestant worshippers. Since then, all 12 stanzas have been mixed and matched in hymnals, with the result that our modern-day version of this hymn is the collaborative effort of two theologically diverse men. Perhaps this irony points to the unified worship Christ will receive in heaven forever.

Words by MATTHEW BRIDGES and GODFREY THRING
Music by GEORGE JOB ELVEY
Arranged by Phillip Keveren

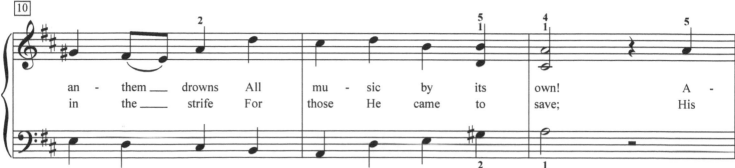

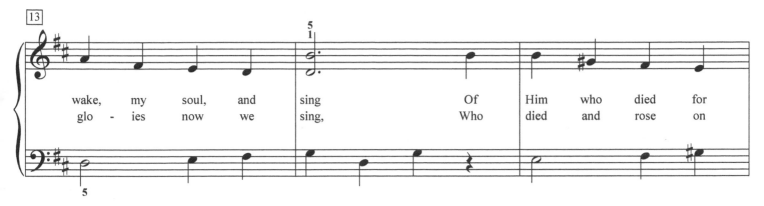

ETERNAL FATHER, STRONG TO SAVE

William Whiting was the master of the Winchester Choristers' school in England from 1842 on. The story goes that a student who had a ticket to sail to America confided in Whiting that he was afraid of the ocean. In response, he wrote these lyrics about God's protection at sea and gave them to the student before he left. John B. Dykes soon after wrote a tune for Whiting's lyrics that he called "Melita," named after the island location of St. Paul's shipwreck in Acts 27. The U.S. and English Navies have especially embraced the hymn, but new verses have been written over the years for travelers of land, air, and outer space. Wherever God's people go, they can know their Watchman never sleeps (Ps. 121).

Words by WILLIAM WHITING
Music by JOHN BACCHUS DYKES
Arranged by Phillip Keveren

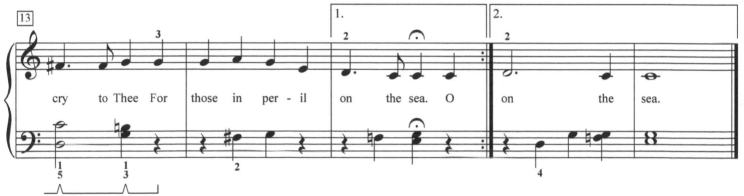

JOY TO THE WORLD

In 1719, Englishman Isaac Watts published a hymnal called *The Psalms of David Imitated in the Language of the New Testament.* In this, he took various psalms and re-wrote them as if David had written them after Christ's first coming. Isaac felt the Old Testament could be better understood in light of its fulfillment in Jesus Christ (Mt. 5:17). He wrote "Joy to the World" as a reinterpretation of Psalm 98, which says, "Shout for joy to the Lord, all the earth… for he comes" (NIV, vv. 4a, 9b). This verse anticipates Christ's first arrival, but we can now say, "The Lord has come and is coming again!" Isaac's lyrics and an arrangement by Lowell Mason that uses parts of Handel's *Messiah* combine to create this jubilant Christmas hymn.

Words by ISAAC WATTS
Music by GEORGE FRIDERIC HANDEL
Adapted by LOWELL MASON
Arranged by Phillip Keveren

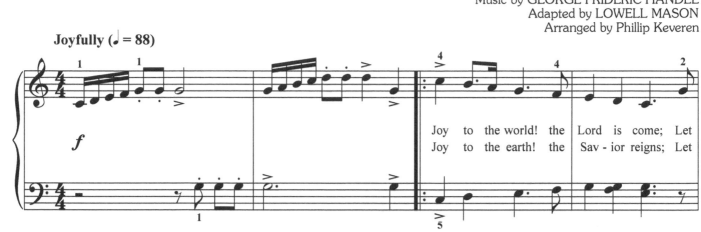

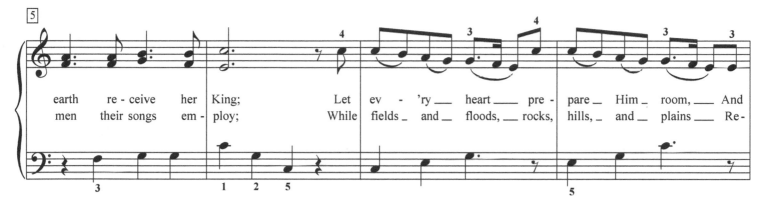

FAIREST LORD JESUS

German Jesuits published this hymn in 1677, though the words have been found in a 1662 manuscript. The original authorship of this hymn is largely a mystery, but many think it was written by persecuted followers of John Hus, a Czech reformer in the early 15th century, who were forced to flee Bohemia and take refuge in Silesia, now a part of modern Poland. These refugees had to keep their beliefs hidden, but they appear to have written and sung many hymns to sustain their faith through difficult times. If this heavily persecuted faction of Christians truly did produce "Fairest Lord Jesus," it is clear their hearts were focused on the right thing: their incomparably glorious Savior, Jesus Christ.

Words from *Münster Gesangbuch*
Music from *Schlesische Volkslieder*
Arranged by Phillip Keveren

Reverently (♩ = 88)

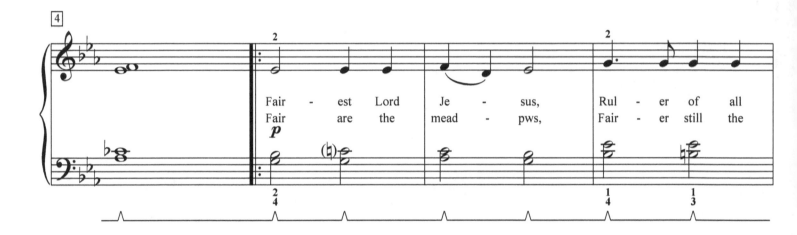

Fair - est Lord Je - sus, Rul - er of all
Fair are the mead - ows, Fair - er still the

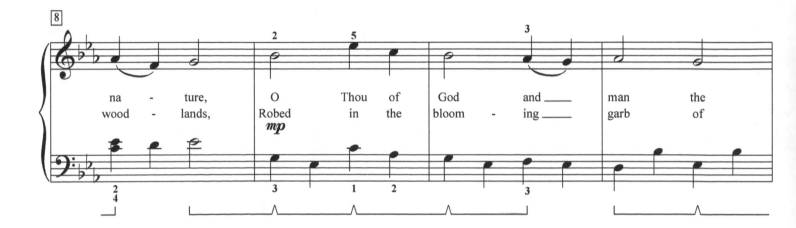

na - ture, O Thou of God and ___ man the
wood - lands, Robed in the bloom - ing ___ garb of

Son;
spring;
Thee will I cher - ish,
Je - sus is fair - er,

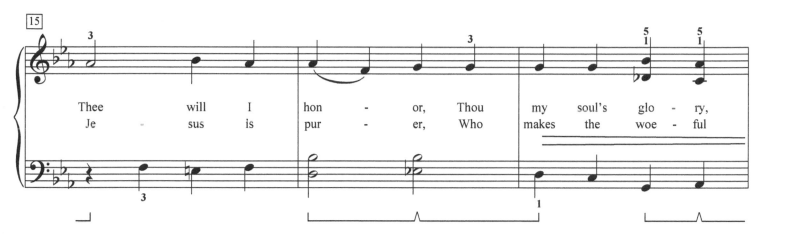

Thee will I hon - or, Thou my soul's glo - ry,
Je - sus is pur - er, Who makes the woe - ful

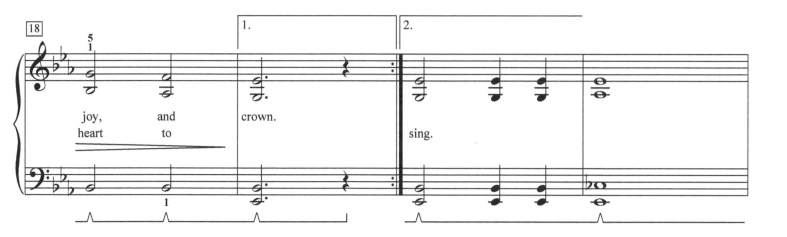

joy, and crown.
heart to sing.

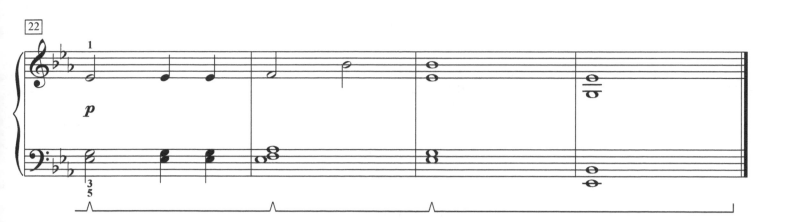

GOD LEADS US ALONG

George A. Young was a carpenter and preacher in the rural Midwest of the United States who had finally saved up enough money to build his family a small cottage. While away on a ministry trip, someone who did not agree with his preaching burned the family's new home to the ground. It is said that, within days, Young had composed both the lyrics and the tune of "God Leads Along." Young knew that following Christ sometimes looks more like "the valley of the shadow of death" than "green pastures" or "still waters" (Ps. 23). However, he knew we do not need to fear what may happen in this dark valley, because God is near and is leading us through whatever may come.

Words and Music by
GEORGE A. YOUNG
Arranged by Phillip Keveren

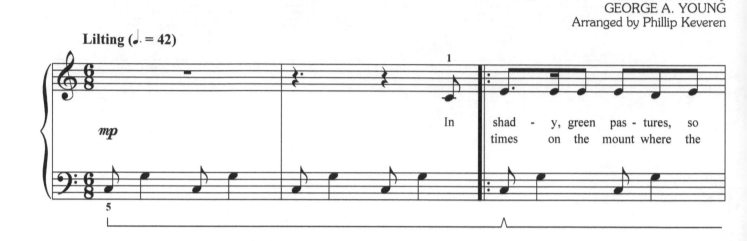

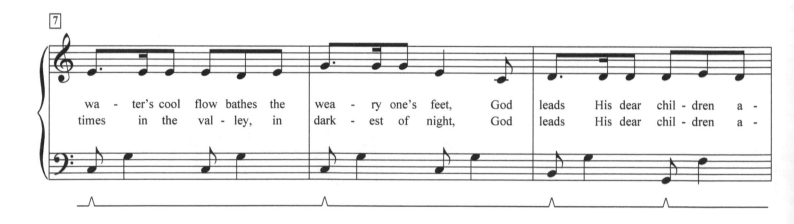

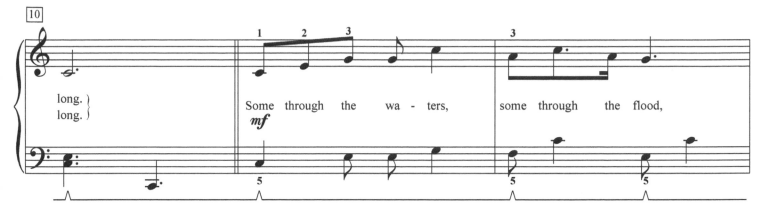

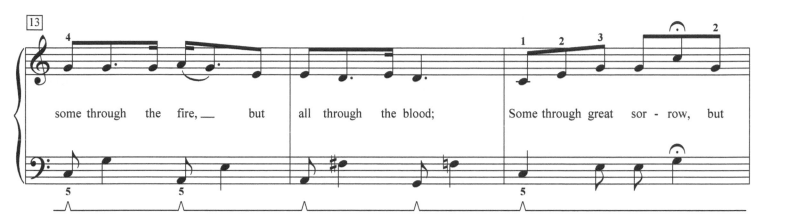

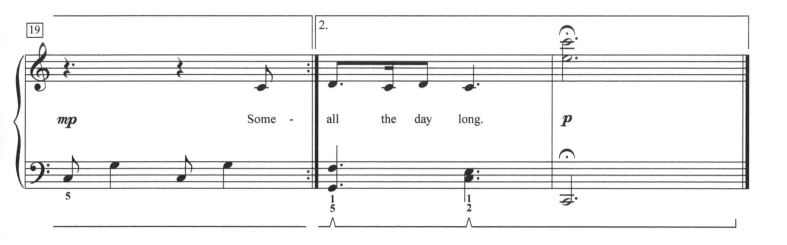

GOD WILL TAKE CARE OF YOU

In 1904, the Martin family was staying at a Bible school in Lestershire, New York. Reverend Walter Martin had been charged with the task of compiling hymns in a songbook for the institution. One Sunday, Walter had a preaching engagement at a church a good distance away. However, his wife Civilla awoke sick, and he thought he must stay home to help her. His young son piped up saying, "Father, don't you think that if God wants you to preach today, He will take care of Mother while you are away?" Walter did preach and when he returned home, Civilla was feeling much better and had written the lyrics of this hymn. Walter composed the hymn's tune later that evening, assured of the truth of its words.

Words by CIVILLA D. MARTIN
Music by WALTER STILLMAN MARTIN
Arranged by Phillip Keveren

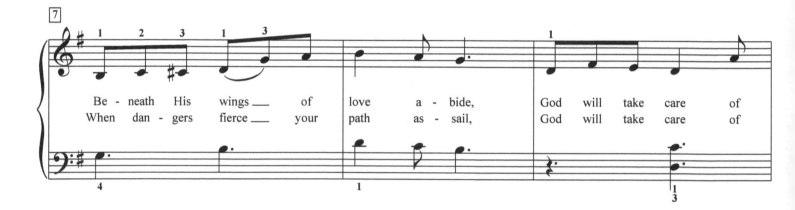

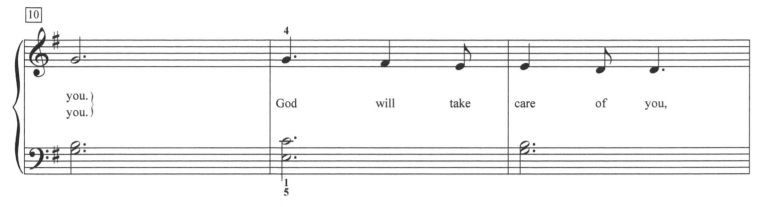

you.}
you.}   God   will   take   care   of   you,

Through ev - 'ry day,   o'er all the way;   He   will   take

care _____ of   you,   God   will   take   care _____ of

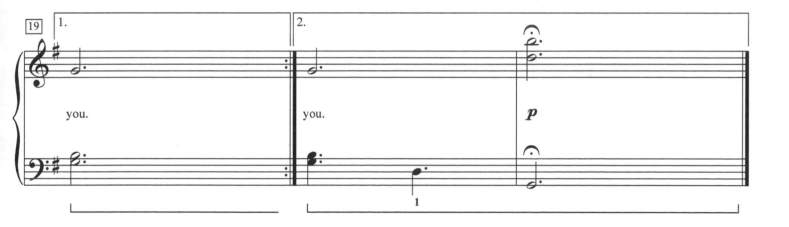

1.   2.
you.   you.   *p*

GUIDE ME, O THOU GREAT JEHOVAH

Born in Wales in 1717, William Williams wrote around 800 hymns in his lifetime. He was to Wales what Charles Wesley was to England in that same time period. As a young doctor-in-training, he converted under the preaching of evangelist Howell Harris and became a minister instead. When accused of misdemeanors against the Church of England in 1744, he embraced Methodism and took to itinerant preaching. He was constantly on the go and faced harsh conditions and people. In 1745, he wrote this hymn. It alludes to God's provision along the Israelites' difficult journey to the Promised Land. Today, this hymn inspires Christians across denominational and national lines to trust in God's sure provision along the narrow road that leads to eternal life (Mt. 7:14).

Words by WILLIAM WILLIAMS
Music by JOHN HUGHES
Arranged by Phillip Keveren

Guide me, O Thou great ___ Je - ho - vah, Pil - grim through this
O - pen now the crys - tal ___ foun - tain, Whence the heal - ing

bar - ren land; I am weak, but Thou ___ art ___ might - y;
stream doth flow; Let the fire and cloud - y ___ pil - lar

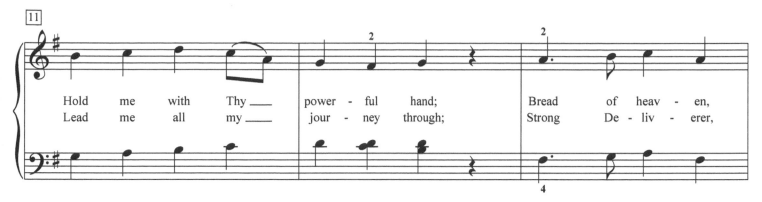

Hold me with Thy ___ power - ful hand;   Bread   of heav - en,
Lead me all my ___ jour - ney through;   Strong   De - liv - erer,

Bread   of heav - en,   Feed   me till I want no   more,
strong   De - liv - erer,   Be   Thou still my strength and   shield,

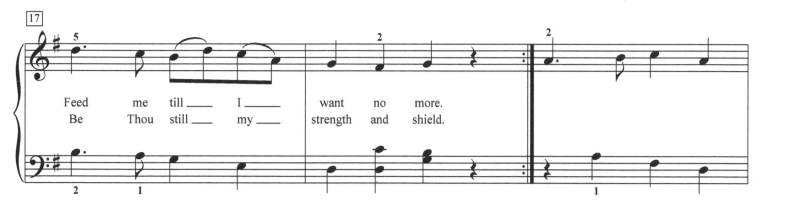

Feed   me till ___ I ___ want no more.
Be   Thou still ___ my ___ strength and shield.

HOLY, HOLY, HOLY

This hymn was written by Reginald Heber, an Anglican clergyman who tragically died of a stroke in 1826 at age 43. It was published posthumously by his widow, along with 56 other hymns he had written. Heber penned "Holy, Holy, Holy" for use in his congregation on Trinity Sunday (eight weeks after Easter). John B. Dykes wrote the tune for it and called it "Nicea," hearkening to the Council of Nicea (A.D. 325) that established the doctrine of the Trinity. This hymn beautifully displays orthodox Christian belief about God's nature, and encourages all who worship Him to do so in wondrous awe. Holy Father, Holy Son, and Holy Spirit: this is the Lord God Almighty who was and is and forever shall be!

Text by REGINALD HEBER
Music by JOHN B. DYKES
Arranged by Phillip Keveren

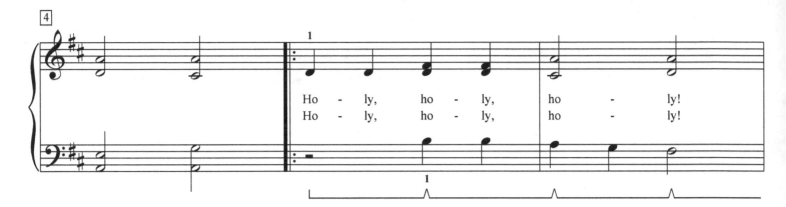

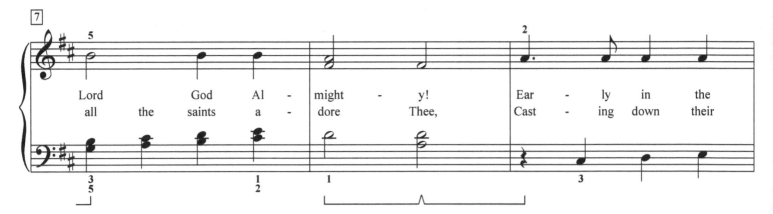

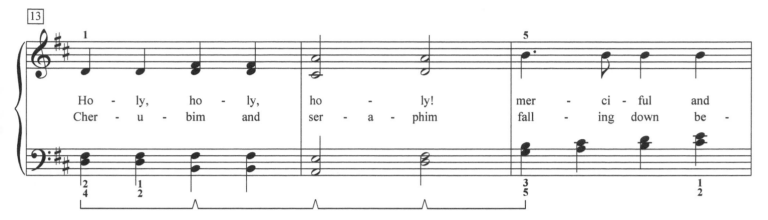

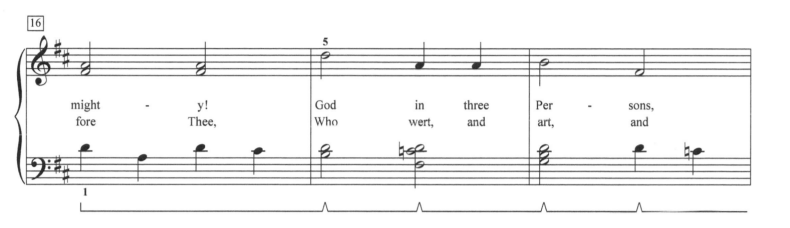

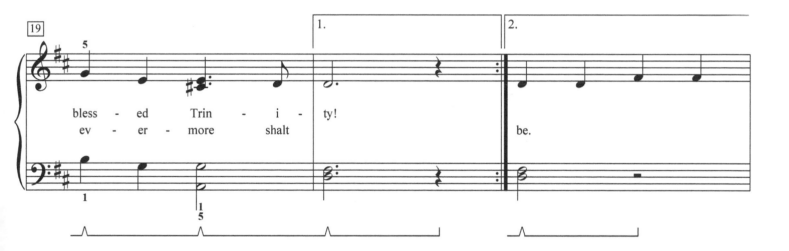

HOW FIRM A FOUNDATION

In 1787, John Rippon, pastor of Carter Lane Baptist Church in London, published *A Selection of Hymns from the Best Authors.*
A hymn called "Exceedingly Great and Precious Promises" was published, but there was no author's name beside it, only the
initial K. The author of the lyrics and/or tune of this hymn, now called "How Firm a Foundation," is a mystery, but one thing
is for sure: the lyricist knew his or her Bible. The first verse states that we can trust God's words in Scripture.
The rest of the hymn is a string of near direct quotations of God's promises in Scripture.
The human origin may not be known, but God is speaking directly to us through this hymn.

Traditional text compiled by JOHN RIPPON
Traditional music compiled by JOSEPH FUNK
Arranged by Phillip Keveren

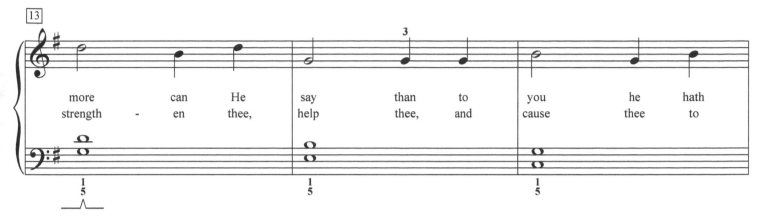

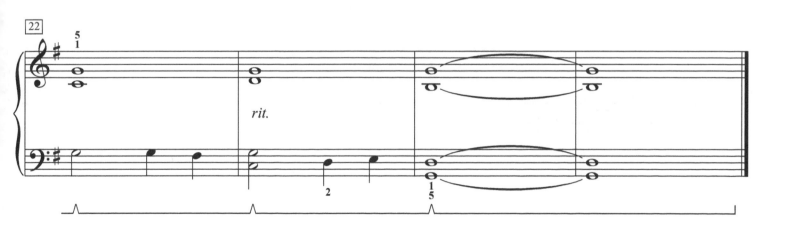

I NEED THEE EVERY HOUR

In John 15, Christ teaches that disciples need Him continually. Perhaps no one knows how much Christ is needed in every moment better than a stay-at-home mom. One June day, Annie Hawks (b. 1835) was joyfully going about her household duties, including the care of her three children, when she was overwhelmed with a tangible sense of Christ's presence. She says that she immediately realized she could never "live without Him, either in joy or pain." Annie wrote a poem and gave it to her pastor, Robert Lowry, who was aware of her poetic gift and had a standing offer with her to write hymn tunes if she would write the lyrics. He kept his word, and this prayer-song was born.

Words by ANNIE S. HAWKS
Music by ROBERT LOWRY
Arranged by Phillip Keveren

I

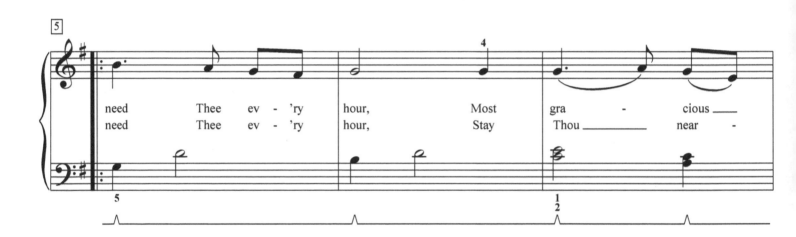

need Thee ev - 'ry hour, Most gra - cious _____
need Thee ev - 'ry hour, Stay Thou _____ near -

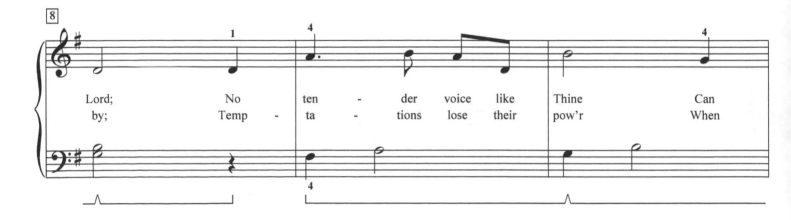

Lord; No ten - der voice like Thine Can
by; Temp - ta - tions lose their pow'r When

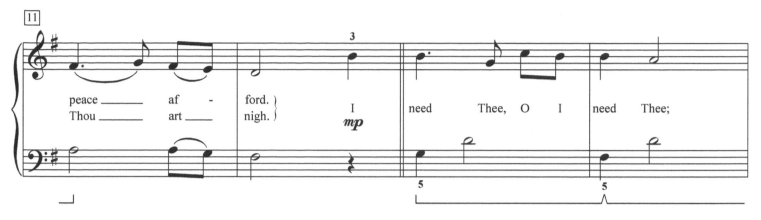

peace _____ af - ford. }
Thou _____ art _____ nigh. }

mp I need Thee, O I need Thee;

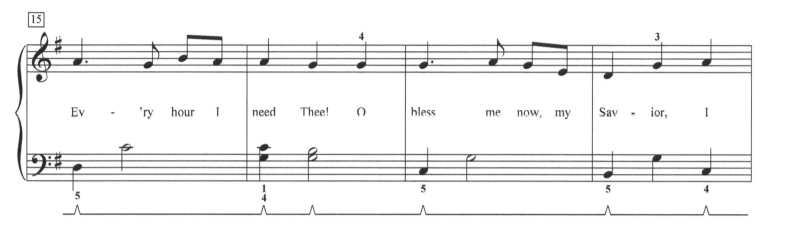

Ev - 'ry hour I need Thee! O bless me now, my Sav - ior, I

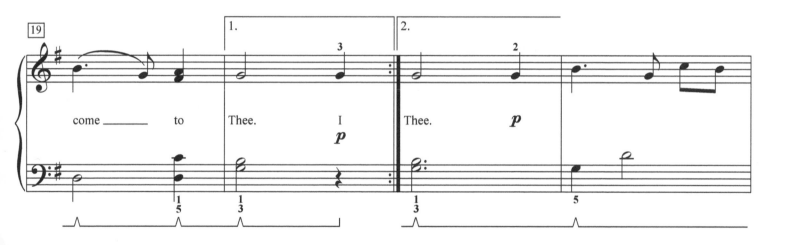

1.
come _____ to Thee. I
p

2.
Thee. *p*

rit.

I SURRENDER ALL

Judson Wheeler Van DeVenter (b. 1855) was a gifted evangelist who traveled all over the United States, England, and Scotland, but early in his life he did not embrace the call God had upon his life. In college, he studied art and music, and he went on to teach art in public schools. He aspired to become an excellent and famous artist. A believer since age 17, Judson was active in the Methodist Episcopal Church, and friends could see he had an unusually great gifting for music evangelism. However, Judson wrestled with God for five years before finally giving everything to Him. At a later time, he wrote the lyrics of this hymn, giving expression to the fully surrendered heart posture God had patiently wrought in him.

Words by J.W. VAN DeVENTER
Music by W.S. WEEDEN
Arranged by Phillip Keveren

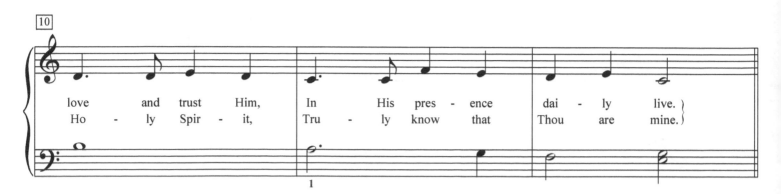

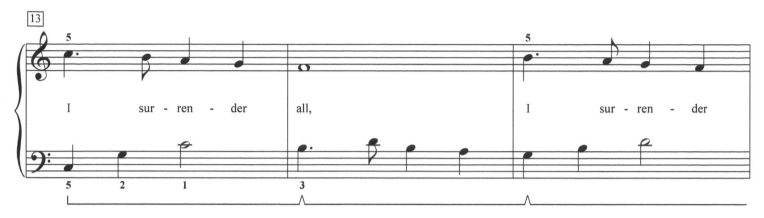

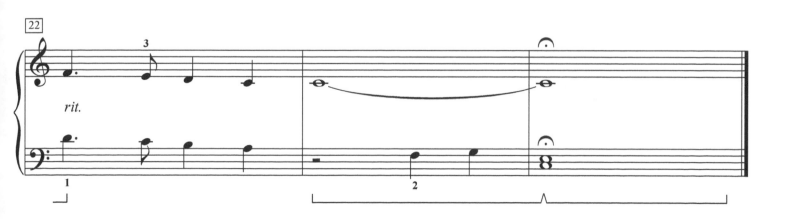

IMMORTAL, INVISIBLE

A minister named Walter Chalmers Smith wrote the words of this hymn while he was the pastor of the Free High Church of Edinburgh, Scotland (c. 1876). The hymn beautifully expresses the "otherness" of God, who is so perfect and holy that no human being can see or approach Him (1 Tim. 6:16). Have you ever flipped on the lights after being in a dark room for a while? It takes time for your eyes to adjust. In Christ, God comes near to us and gradually helps our eyes and hearts adjust to seeing and knowing Him as He really is (Jn. 1:18). Now we see dimly, but one day we will gaze upon His ineffable glory face-to-face (1 Cor. 13:12).

Words by WALTER CHALMERS SMITH
Traditional Welsh Melody
From John Roberts' *Canaidau y Cyssegr*
Arranged by Phillip Keveren

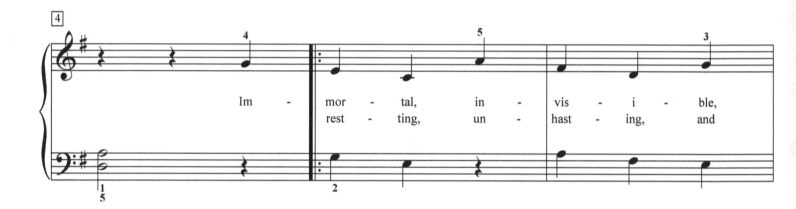

Im - mor - tal, in - vis - i - ble,
rest - ing, un - hast - ing, and

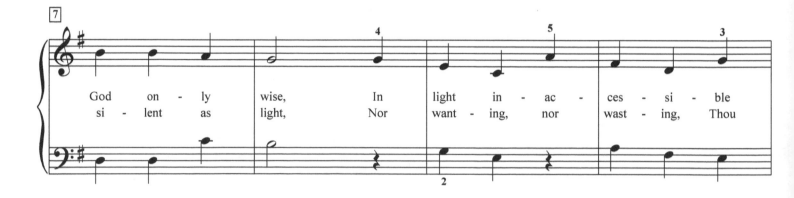

God on - ly wise, In light in - ac - ces - si - ble
si - lent as light, Nor want - ing, nor wast - ing, Thou

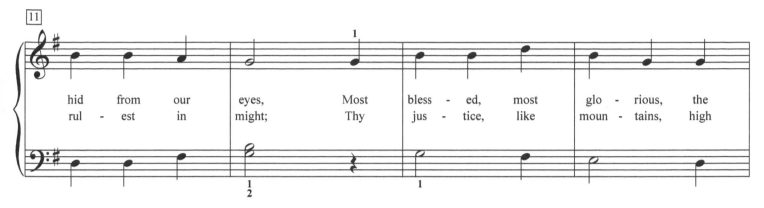

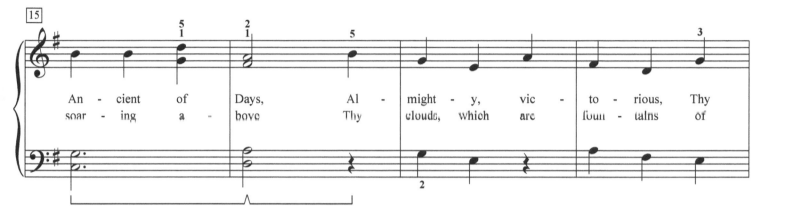

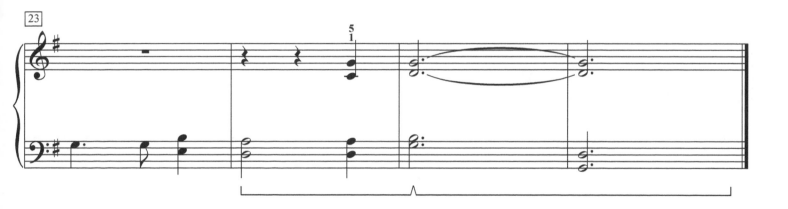

IN THE GARDEN

Charles Austin Miles was a pharmacist turned hymn writer and church music director. Also an amateur photographer, he kept his organ and Bible in the dark room so he could have private devotional time while film was developing. One day in March 1912, as he meditated on his favorite passage, John 20, about Mary Magdalene's encounter with the risen Christ, the Scripture came alive to him in a new way. It was almost as if he were witnessing the garden scene on a movie screen. Shaken by the beauty of this experience, Miles immediately wrote the words of this hymn and composed the tune that evening. This hymn reminds us that those who seek Jesus see and hear Him best in the quiet, "in the garden alone."

Words and Music by
CHARLES AUSTIN MILES
Arranged by Phillip Keveren

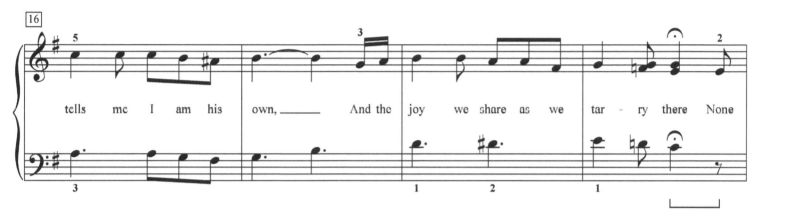

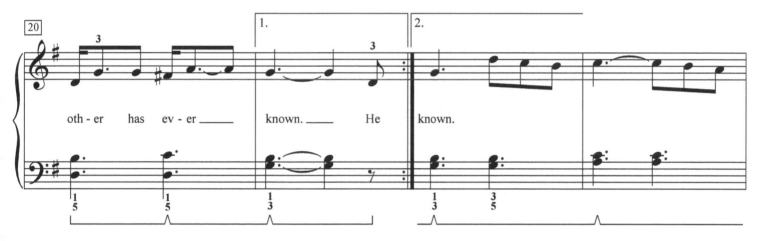

IT IS WELL WITH MY SOUL

A successful lawyer with a large family, Horatio Spafford lost nearly everything within two years (1871-73). His son died, most of his real estate investments were destroyed, and then his four daughters drowned in a shipwreck on their way to Europe. Upon receiving the news, Horatio immediately sailed to Europe to meet his wife, who had survived the tragedy. En route, the captain pointed out the general area where the shipwreck had occurred. In a way reminiscent of Job's "The Lord gave and the Lord has taken away; may the name of the Lord be praised" (NIV, Job 1:21b), Horatio said, "It is well; may the will of God be done." He later wrote the lyrics of this hymn based on his faith-filled response to unthinkable suffering.

Words by HORATIO G. SPAFFORD
Music by PHILIP P. BLISS
Arranged by Phillip Keveren

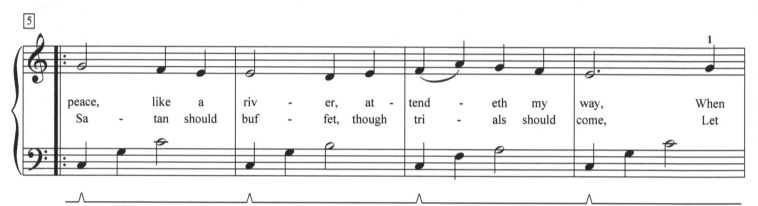

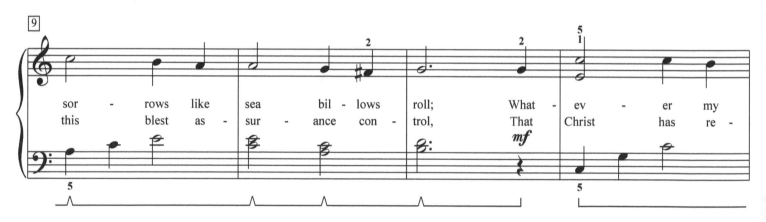

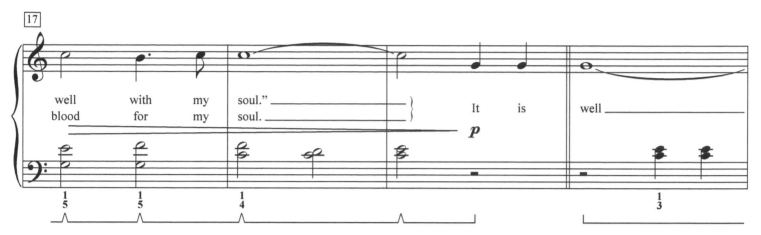

well with my soul."
blood for my soul.

It is well

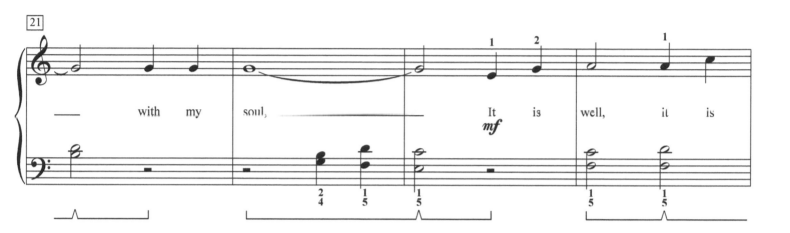

with my soul,

It is well, it is

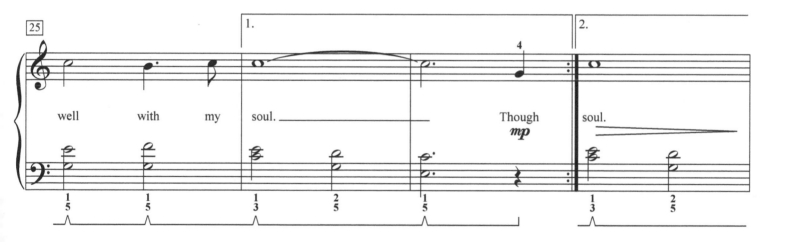

well with my soul.

Though

soul.

rit.

JESUS, LOVER OF MY SOUL

Psalm 34:19 states, "The righteous person may have many troubles, but the Lord delivers him from them all" (NIV).
Charles Wesley certainly knew what it meant to encounter troubles and to need God's deliverance out of them. He spent much
of his life in itinerant preaching, not knowing if his next audience would experience the Holy Spirit's conviction or try to kill him. In
Psalm 91:14, God says, "Because he loves me… I will rescue him; I will protect him, for he acknowledges my name" (NIV). It is
a good thing Charles both loved God and was confident in God's love for him, even able to call Jesus the "Lover" of his soul.
In this intimate Love relationship, there is refuge in this life and bliss eternally.

Words by CHARLES WESLEY
Music by SIMEON B. MARSH
Arranged by Phillip Keveren

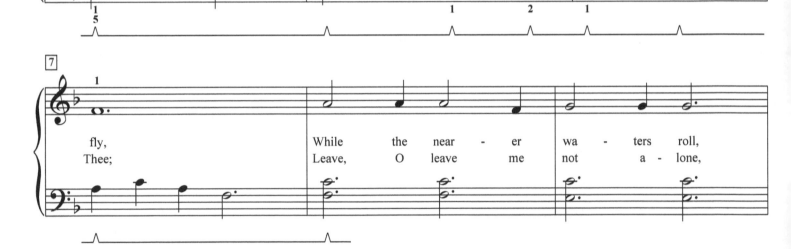

Hide me, O my Sav - ior, hide,
All my trust on Thee is stayed,

Till the storm of life is past;
All my help of from Thee I bring;

Safe in - to the ha - ven guide; O re - ceive my
Cov - er my de - fense - less head With the shad - ow

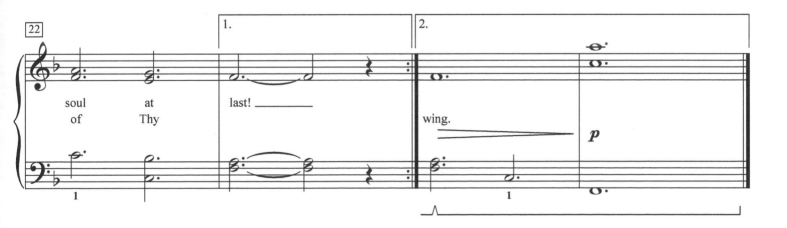

soul at last! _____
of Thy

wing.

JESUS PAID IT ALL

One Sunday in 1865, a woman named Elvina Hall was sitting in the choir loft at Monument Street Methodist Church in Baltimore, Maryland. The pastor's prayer was lengthy that morning, and she found her mind beginning to muse on other things. She began to write a poem about Christ's all-sufficient work in the flyleaf of her hymnal. Perhaps embarrassed that her mind had wandered during his prayer, Elvina was still convinced she needed to share her poem with the pastor. The choir director, John Grape, had recently composed a tune he called "All to Christ I Owe" and had also shared it with the pastor. The pastor recommended that the tune and poem be put together, and they fit perfectly, producing this moving hymn.

Words by ELVINA M. HALL
Music by JOHN T. GRAPE
Arranged by Phillip Keveren

Je - sus paid it all, All to Him I

owe; Sin had left a crim - son stain, He

washed it white as snow. Lord, ___ snow.

rit.

JOYFUL, JOYFUL WE ADORE THEE

Henry Van Dyke was a Presbyterian minister who became a professor of English literature at Princeton University. In 1907, he was scheduled to preach at Williams College in Massachusetts. During his stay there, he was inspired to write the words of this hymn while gazing upon the beauty of the local Berkshire Mountains. He reportedly handed the president of the school a piece of paper with the new lyrics and the instruction to sing them with Beethoven's "Hymn to Joy." The hymn is rich with imagery of the creation that continually declares "the glory of God" (NIV, Ps. 19:1a). When God's people see the beauty of what He has made, they often can't help but smell wafts of Eden and joyfully anticipate the new heaven and earth.

Words by HENRY VAN DYKE
Music by LUDWIG VAN BEETHOVEN,
melody from Ninth Symphony
Arranged by Phillip Keveren

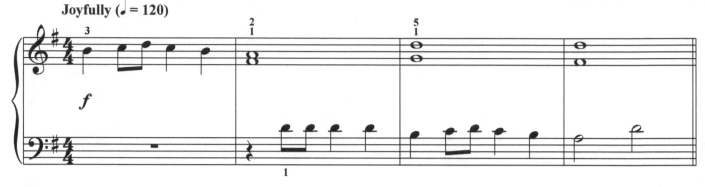

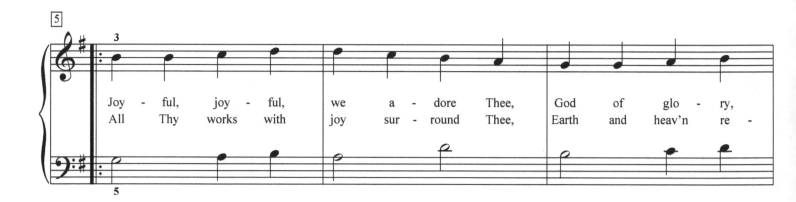

Joy - ful, joy - ful, we a - dore Thee, God of glo - ry,
All Thy works with joy sur - round Thee, Earth and heav'n re -

Lord of love; Hearts un - fold like flowers be - fore Thee,
flect Thy rays, Stars and an - gels sing a - round Thee,

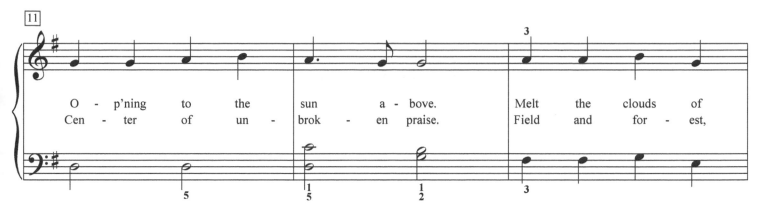

O - p'ning to the sun a - bove.
Cen - ter of un - brok - en praise.

Melt the clouds of

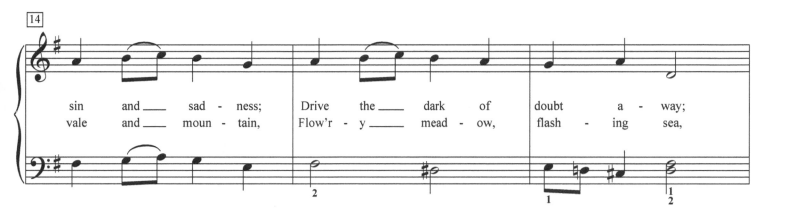

sin and __ sad - ness;
vale and __ moun - tain,

Drive the __ dark of
Flow'r - y __ mead - ow,

doubt a - way;
flash - ing sea,

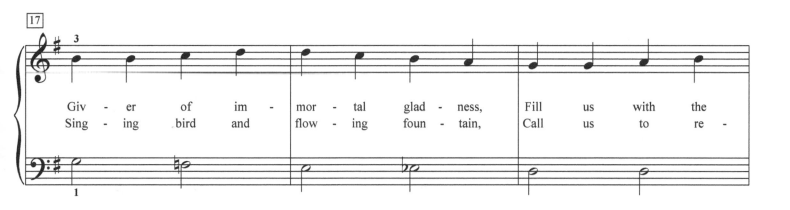

Giv - er of im - mor - tal glad - ness,
Sing - ing bird and flow - ing foun - tain,

Fill us with the
Call us to re -

light of day!
joice in Thee!

JUST AS I AM

Before becoming a Christian, Charlotte Elliot was unhappily struggling with chronic physical illness and disability. In 1822, a minister named Cesar Malan told her that Jesus Christ could cure her bitterness. She was put off at first, but the thought began to make sense to her, and she later asked the minister how she could come to Christ. He told her to come just as she was, without first trying to fix herself. She did. She wrote this hymn text years later, at a time when her disabilities left her feeling useless to God, to bolster her faith in his unconditional love. This hymn has helped countless thousands to come to faith, assured that whoever comes to Jesus will never be sent away (Jn. 6:37).

Words by CHARLOTTE ELLIOTT
Music by WILLIAM B. BRADBURY
Arranged by Phillip Keveren

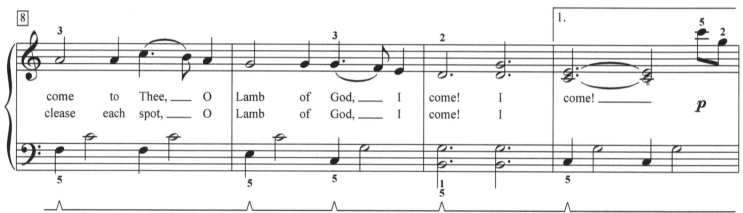

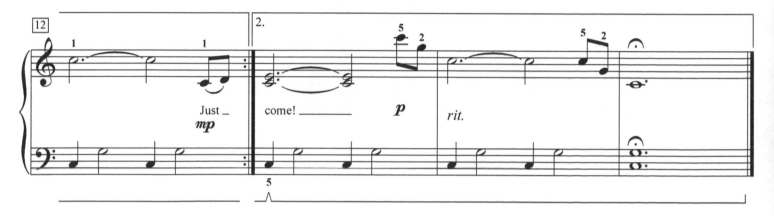

LET US BREAK BREAD TOGETHER ⁶¹

This hymn was forged in the lives of 18th-19th century African-American slaves and was passed down orally, finally being published in 1927. The lyrics speak of breaking bread, drinking wine, and praising God while kneeling. As a result, it has often been used as a Communion hymn. Communion also anticipates the Second Coming of Christ (1 Cor. 11:26), so many hymnologists have seen in the hymn's mention of "face to the rising sun" the hope of the new day that will dawn with Christ's return. It would certainly make sense that African slaves would have been focused on the promise of a just human society in God's coming Kingdom. In response to this yearning, Jesus says, "Yes, I am coming soon" (NIV, Rev. 22:20b).

Traditional Spiritual
Arranged by Phillip Keveren

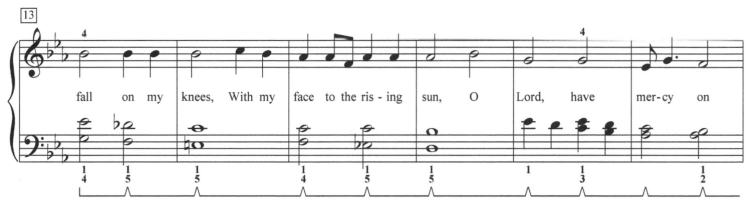

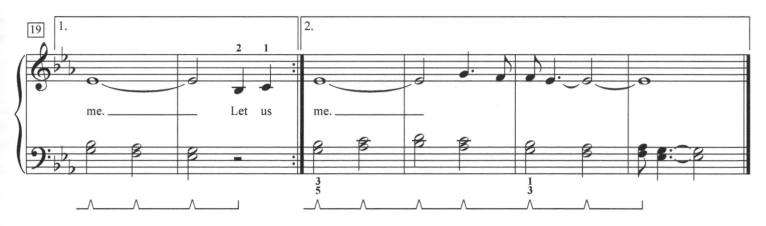

THE LORD'S MY SHEPHERD, I'LL NOT WANT

The book of Psalms is the only comprehensive collection of worship and praise songs in the Bible. Though most English translations of psalms do not easily lend themselves to singing, the Church of Scotland produced excellent, singable English versions of all 150 psalms. In preparation for the publication of their *Scottish Psalter* (1650), committees of Biblical scholars pored over each psalm to ensure that their metrical English translations remained faithful to the original Hebrew. "The Lord's My Shepherd," Psalm 23, has emerged as the favorite from this collection. John Calvin once said about Biblical psalms, "We shall not find better songs… when we sing them, we are certain that God puts in our mouths these, as if He Himself were singing in us to exalt His glory."

Words from *Scottish Psalter*, 1650
Based on Psalm 23
Music by JESSIE S. IRVINE
Arranged by Phillip Keveren

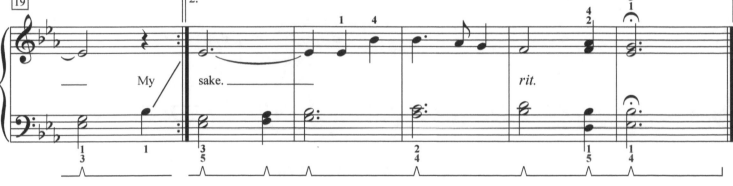

MY FAITH LOOKS UP TO THEE

In 1830, 22-year-old Ray Palmer was exhausted from his school and work loads. One night, he wrote an emotional prayer-poem in his journal, asking Jesus to strengthen him to love and serve only Him for the rest of his days. Two years later, Lowell Mason, who was building his music career, wanted to publish a new hymnbook. He asked Palmer, now a ministry student, if he had anything to contribute. Palmer showed him the poem from his journal. Mason loved it and composed a tune for it that evening. He reportedly later said to Palmer, "You may live many years and do many good things, but I think you will be best known to posterity as the author of 'My Faith Looks Up to Thee.'"

Words by RAY PALMER
Music by LOWELL MASON
Arranged by Phillip Keveren

LOVE DIVINE, ALL LOVES EXCELLING

Charles Wesley wrote thousands of hymn texts, many of them conceived while he was on horseback, traveling to his next ministry appointment. He would often hurriedly scribble verses down on the first piece of paper he could find after dismounting at his destination. This particular hymn text is a prayer to Jesus for salvation, not just in the initial sense of conversion but also in the sense of deliverance from sin and reception of the fullness of the Holy Spirit. Charles knew that full salvation would be experienced only in the next life, but he believed God's Divine Love was powerful enough to create holy people, sanctified lovers, to serve Him wholeheartedly in this world.

Words by CHARLES WESLEY
Music by JOHN ZUNDEL
Arranged by Phillip Keveren

mer - cies __ crown! Je - sus, Thou art all com - pas - sion, Pure, un - bound - ed
prom - ised __ rest. Take a - way our bent to __ sin - ning; Al - pha and O -

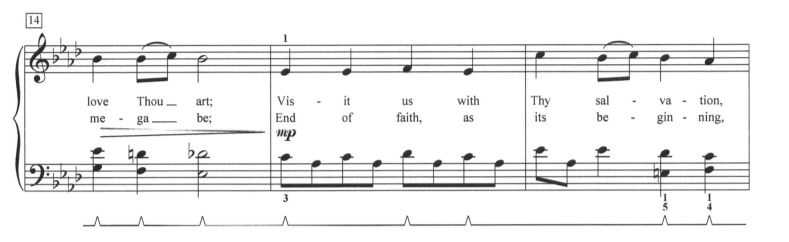

love Thou __ art; Vis - it us with Thy sal - va - tion,
me - ga __ be; End of faith, as its be - gin - ning,

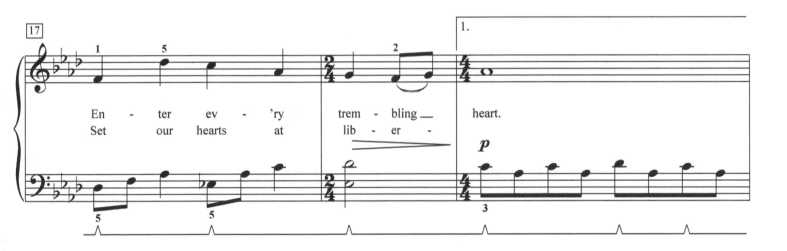

En - ter ev - 'ry trem - bling __ heart.
Set our hearts at lib - er -

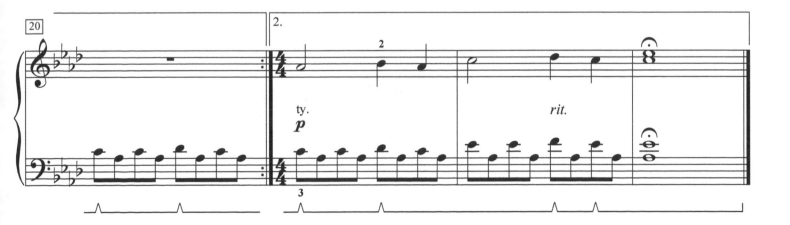

ty.

A MIGHTY FORTRESS IS OUR GOD

In 1517, when Martin Luther nailed his 95 Theses to the church door in Wittenburg, Germany, he had little idea how great a battle his document would spark. Though he wrote his Theses with the hope of reforming the Roman Catholic Church from within, Luther soon found himself excommunicated by the Pope (1521). Unabated, Luther and those who followed him risked their lives to form their own churches. Between 1527-29, Luther wrote this hymn, which helped the "Protestants" to remember that if they took refuge in God, Jesus Christ would win the spiritual battle in which they were entangled.

Words and Music by MARTIN LUTHER
Translated by FREDERICK H. HEDGE
Based on Psalm 46
Arranged by Phillip Keveren

mor - tal ills pre-vail - ing. For still our an-cient foe Doth
Man of God's own choos - ing: Dost ask who that may be? Christ

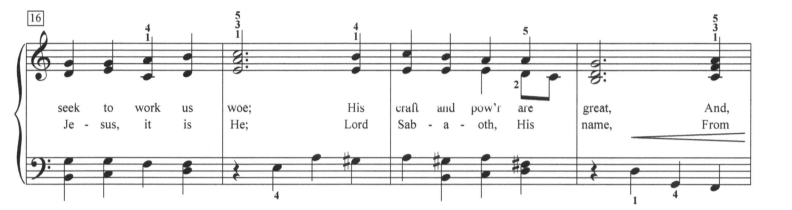

seek to work us woe; His craft and pow'r are great, And,
Je - sus, it is He; His Lord Sab - a - oth, His name, From

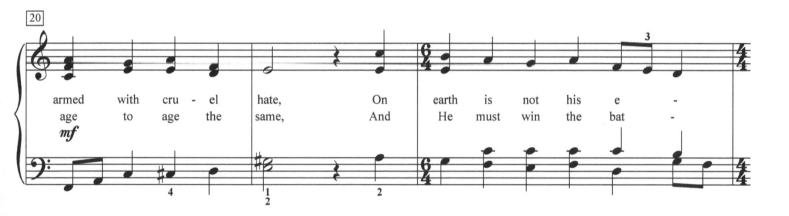

armed with cru-el hate, On earth is not his e -
age to age the same, And He must win the bat -

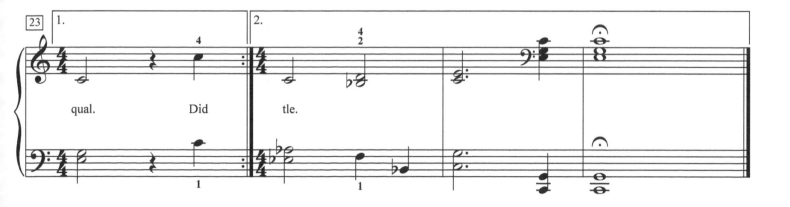

qual. Did
tle.

NEARER, MY GOD, TO THEE

Two sisters are responsible for the writing of this comforting hymn that reportedly was played on the Titanic as it was sinking. Sarah Adams, a young actress who retired early due to declining health, wrote the hymn text based on the story of Jacob's dream in Genesis 28:10-22. Her sister Eliza wrote the original melody, but a tune by Lowell Mason is currently used. This hymn teaches that nothing can separate us from God (Rom. 8:38-39). Even death itself is just the means of becoming fully united with Him in heaven. If we let Him, God will use all of life's experiences, good and bad, to draw us nearer to Himself. "No pit is so deep that God is not deeper still" (Corrie ten Boom).

Words by SARAH F. ADAMS
Based on Genesis 28:10-22
Music by LOWELL MASON
Arranged by Phillip Keveren

Near - er, my God, to Thee, Near - er to
There let the way ap - pear, Steps un - to

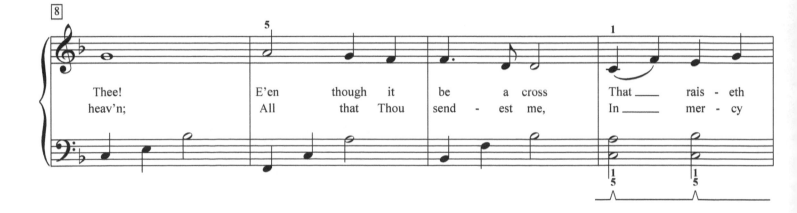

Thee! E'en though it be a cross That ___ rais - eth
heav'n; All that Thou send - est me, In ___ mer - cy

O COME, ALL YE FAITHFUL
(Adeste Fideles)

During the English Jacobite rebellion in 1745, John Francis Wade, an English Catholic layman, was forced from his country, and he found refuge in France. There, he busied himself teaching music and copying musical scores. Around this time, Wade wrote both the text and the tune of a Latin Christmas hymn that circulated the many Catholic refugee communities. When it was safe for English Catholics to return to their homeland, they brought this hymn with them. A century later, Frederick Oakeley, an Anglican minister turned Catholic priest, translated the hymn text into English, calling it "O Come, All Ye Faithful." This Christmas hymn comes to us out of the ruins of political and religious division and invites all faithful believers to worship our one King in unity.

Music by JOHN FRANCIS WADE
Latin Words translated by FREDERICK OAKELEY
Arranged by Phillip Keveren

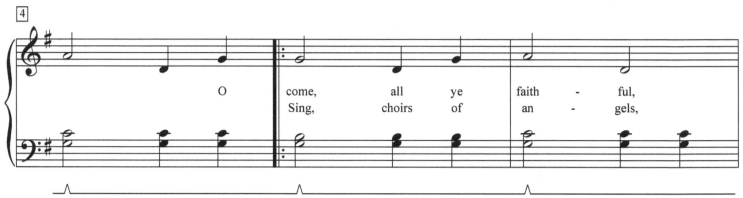

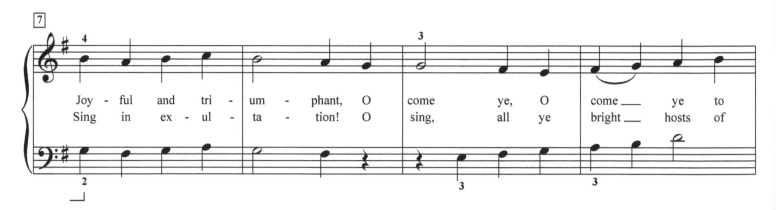

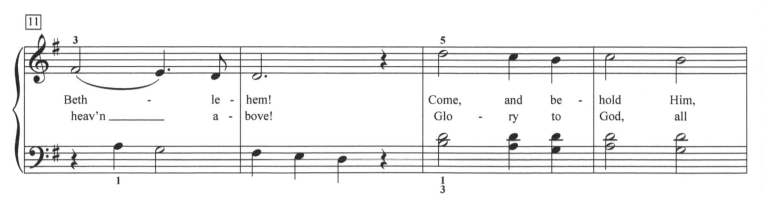

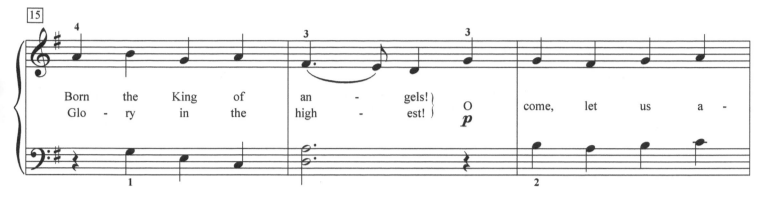

Born the King of an - gels!⎫
Glo - ry in the high - est!⎭ O come, let us a -

dore Him, O come, let us a - dore Him, O come, let us a -

dore Him, ___ Christ ___ the Lord!

Lord!
rit.

O FOR A THOUSAND TONGUES TO SING

In 1739, a year after his transformative conversion experience, Charles Wesley wrote an 18-stanza hymn text he called "For the Anniversary Day of One's Conversion." What was the seventh stanza has now been made the first, and only four or five of the original verses of the hymn, now called "O for a Thousand Tongues to Sing," appear in modern hymnals.
The melody is an arrangement by Lowell Mason of a tune called "Azmon," by Carl G. Glaser, a contemporary of Beethoven.
It is believed that the first line of this hymn was inspired by Charles's mentor, Moravian missionary
Peter Bohler, who once declared, "Had I a thousand tongues, I would praise Him with them all!"

Words by CHARLES WESLEY
Music by CARL G. GLASER
Arranged by LOWELL MASON
Arranged by Phillip Keveren

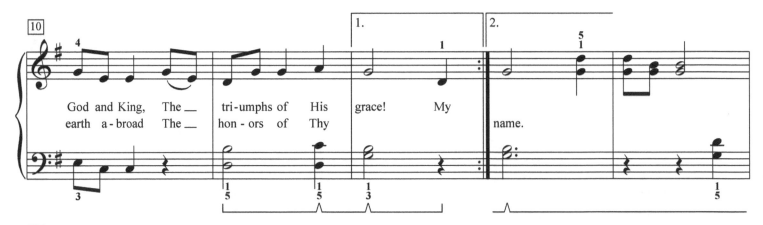

PRAISE GOD, FROM WHOM ALL BLESSINGS FLOW
(Doxology)

When Thomas Ken was orphaned as a young boy, his half-sister and her husband took him in. They sent him to Winchester, a school for boys. After attending Oxford and being ordained as an Anglican clergyman, he returned to Winchester as a chaplain. It is here that he wrote and published hymns for the students to sing at various occasions in their spiritual lives. The last verse of three of his hymns, called Morning, Evening, and Midnight Hymns, is the Doxology we use today. Thomas Ken is thought to be England's first hymn writer, because prior to the circulation of his hymns, only the psalms were sung in congregational worship. Today, his Doxology is perhaps the most widely sung of any hymn ever written.

Words by THOMAS KEN
Music Attributed to LOUIS BOURGEOIS
Arranged by Phillip Keveren

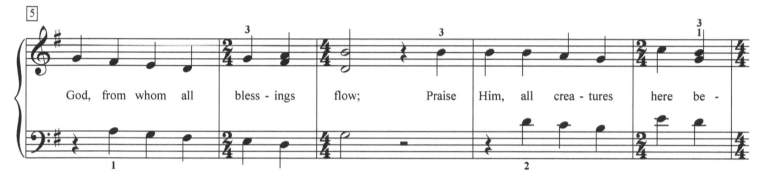

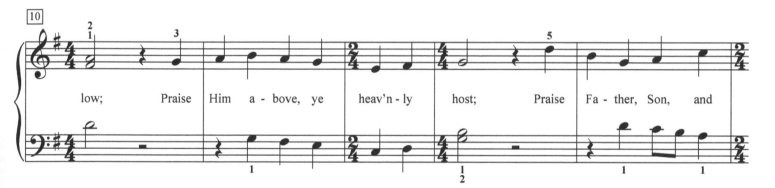

O WORSHIP THE KING

Robert Grant's father, a committed Anglican, directed the East India Company and later joined Parliament. Robert grew up in the political power center of England and eventually served in Parliament himself (1818). While holding this position, he was inspired by Psalm 104 to write this hymn text, using the analogy of earthly royalty to understand God's greatness. The Lord wears light itself and inhabits the whole heavens (vs. 2). God's Spirit empowers human beings to do His bidding, but He could even use the wind or fire to do His will instead (vv. 3-4). The kings and rulers of the earth deserve respect, but infinitely greater honor and unrivaled worship is due the King of kings.

Words by ROBERT GRANT
Music attributed to JOHANN MICHAEL HAYDN
Arranged by Phillip Keveren

With majesty (♩ = 108)

wor - ship the King, all glo - rious a - bove, And
tell of His might, O sing of His grace, Whose

grate - ful - ly sing His won - der - ful love; Our
robe is the light, whose can - o - py space! His

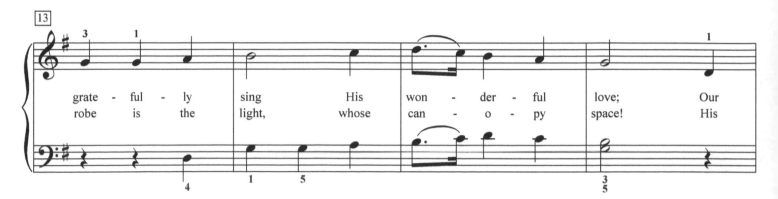

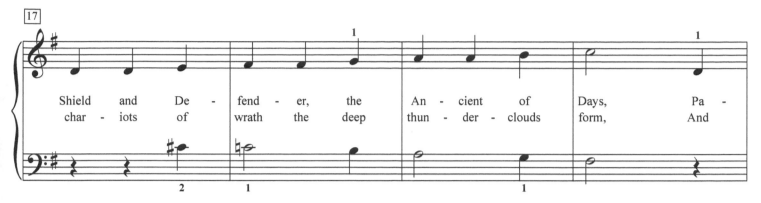

Shield and De - fend - er, the An - cient of Days, Pa -
char - iots of wrath the deep thun - der - clouds form, And

vil - ioncd in splen - dor and gird - ed with praise. O
dark is His path on the wings of the

1.

2.

storm.

rit.

THE OLD RUGGED CROSS

In 1912, George Bennard, a traveling evangelist for the Methodist Episcopal Church, encountered difficulty while trying to convert some rebellious youth at a revival meeting in Michigan. Their disregard for the Gospel and their disrespectful attitude toward George left him hungry for a deeper understanding of Christ's work on the cross. Over the course of several months, he wrote both the words and the melody of "The Old Rugged Cross." The cross is the symbol of Christ's atoning death for all people, but it is also the symbol of self-sacrifice on the road of discipleship (Mt. 6:24). Bennard, in both senses, was determined to "cling to the old rugged cross," knowing eternal life awaited him in exchange.

Words and Music by
REV. GEORGE BENNARD
Arranged by Phillip Keveren

Reverently (♩ = 96)

On a

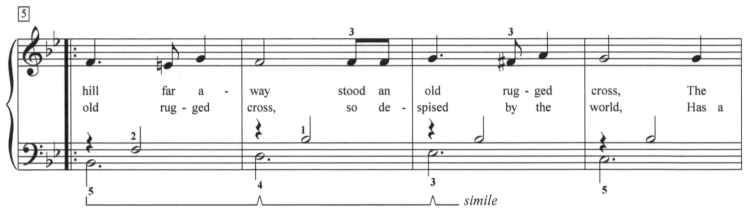

hill far a - way stood an old rug - ged cross, The
old rug - ged cross, so de - spised by the world, Has a

simile

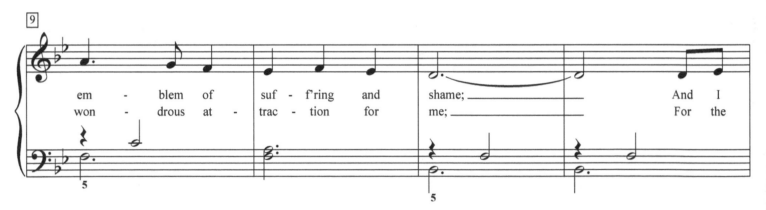

em - blem of suf - f'ring and shame; And I
won - drous at - trac - tion for me; For the

love that old cross, where the dear - est and best For a
dear Lamb of God left His glo - ry a - bove To

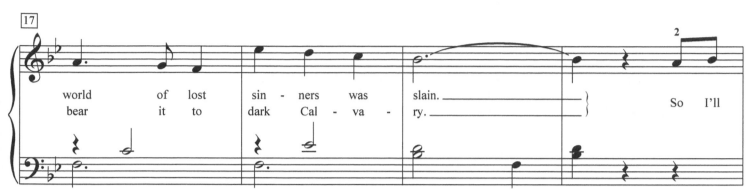

world of lost sin - ners was slain. _____ So I'll
bear it to dark Cal - va - ry. _____

cher - ish the old rug - ged cross, _____ Till my tro - phies at

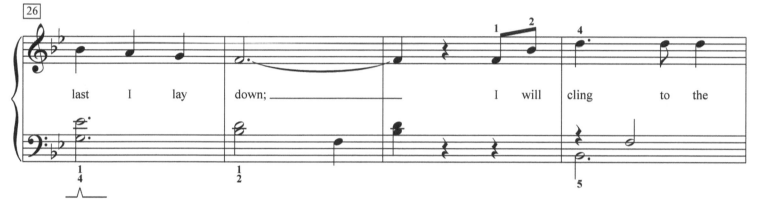

last I lay down; _____ I will cling to the

old rug - ged cross, _____ And ex - change it some -

1.
day for a crown. _____ Oh, that
2.
crown. _____

PRAISE HIM! PRAISE HIM!

At the age of eight, blind Fanny Crosby wrote a poem containing these lines:
"Oh, what a happy soul I am/Although I cannot see/I am resolved that in this world/Contented I will be." She wrote the
lyrics of "Praise Him! Praise Him!" in her forties, perhaps as a reflection of the many exhortations in the psalms to praise God,
but most certainly as an overflow of her own heart-posture of thankfulness and joy. As perhaps the most prolific hymn writer in
all of history, one could see Psalm 146:2b coming straight from Fanny's lips: "I will sing praise to my God as long as I live" (NIV).

Words by FANNY J. CROSBY
Music by CHESTER G. ALLEN
Arranged by Phillip Keveren

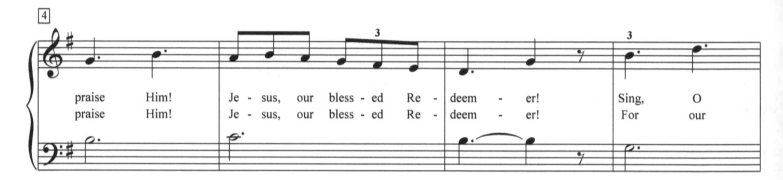

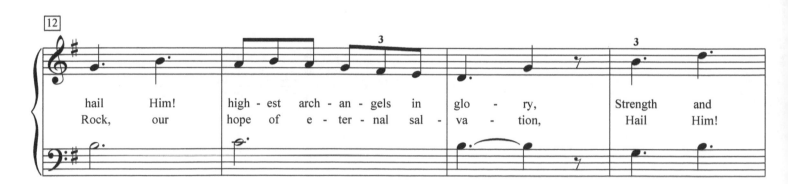

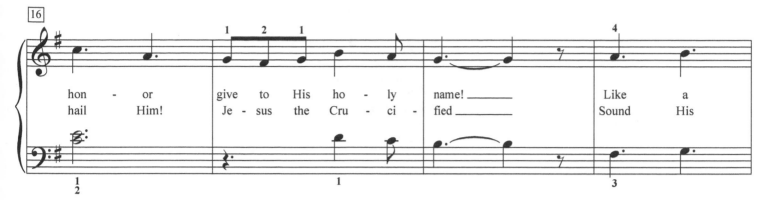

hon - or give to His ho - ly name! _____ Like a
hail Him! Je - sus the Cru - ci - fied _____ Sound His

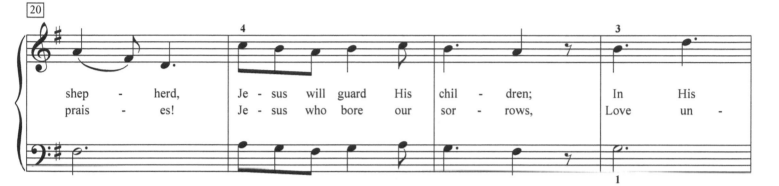

shep - herd, Je - sus will guard His chil - dren; In His
prais - es! Je - sus who bore our sor - rows, Love un -

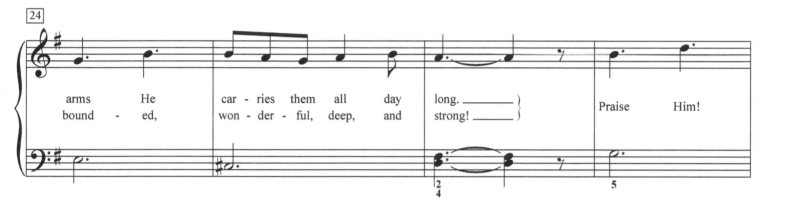

arms He car - ries them all day long. _____ Praise Him!
bound - ed, won - der - ful, deep, and strong! _____ Praise Him!

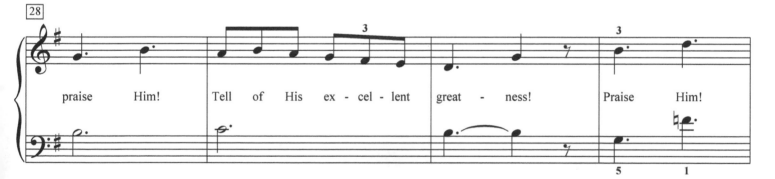

praise Him! Tell of His ex - cel - lent great - ness! Praise Him!

praise Him! ev - er in joy - ful song! _____ song! _____

PRAISE TO THE LORD, THE ALMIGHTY

Joachim Neander (b. 1650) came from three generations of preachers, but he lived a lawless existence until a sudden conversion experience as a young man. After this, he latched onto the German Pietistic movement, which emphasized the experience of a relationship with Jesus Christ instead of the theological dogmatism that seemed to be drying up the vigor of the post-Reformation churches. Before an early death from tuberculosis at the age of 30, Neander produced around 60 hymns. He reportedly wrote the lyrics of "Praise to the Lord, the Almighty" the year he died. How beautiful to God must the sound of praises be from those who believe their sufferings are not worth comparing to the hope they have in Him (Rom. 8:18).

Words by JOACHIM NEANDER
Translated by CATHERINE WINKWORTH
Music from *Erneuerten Gesangbuch*
Arranged by Phillip Keveren

Majestically (♩ = 126)

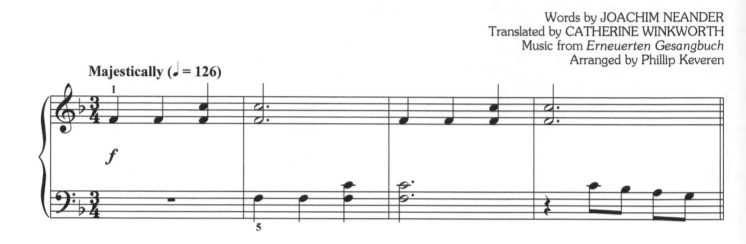

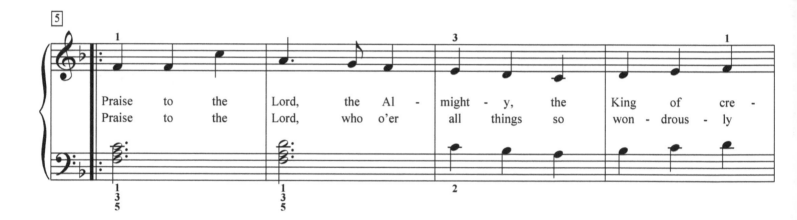

Praise to the Lord, the Al - might - y, the King of cre -
Praise to the Lord, who o'er all things so won - drous - ly

a - tion! O my soul, praise Him for
reign - eth, Shel - ters there un - der His

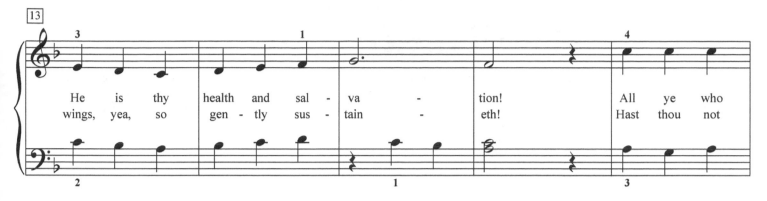

He is thy health and sal - va - tion! All ye who
wings, yea, so gen - tly sus - tain - eth! Hast thou not

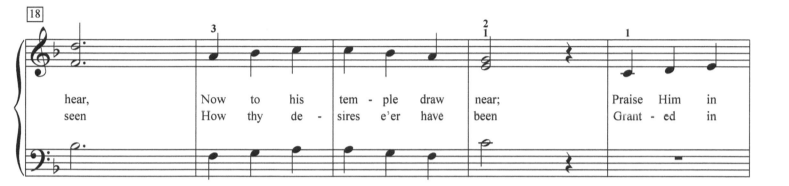

hear, Now to his tem - ple draw near; Praise Him in
seen How thy de - sires e'er have been Grant - ed in

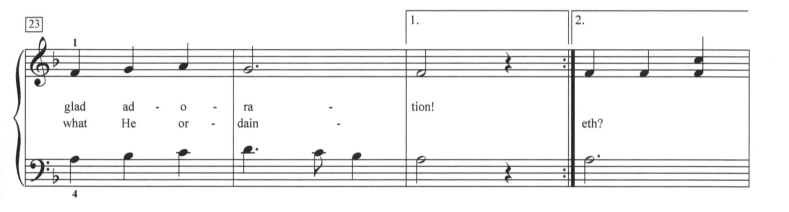

1.

2.

glad ad - o - ra - tion!
what He or - dain - eth? eth?

SAVIOR, LIKE A SHEPHERD LEAD US

In 1836, Dorothy A. Thrupp published a compilation of hymns for children called *Hymns for the Young.* "Savior, Like a Shepherd Lead Us" was included, and though no one knows for sure who wrote the lyrics, many attribute them to Dorothy. The tune was written by William Bradbury, who is also well known for writing the tune to "Jesus Loves Me." Children often readily latch on to the image of Jesus shepherding and carrying His little lambs, but adults do too, thus the popularity of this hymn with Christians of all ages. With Jesus leading and guiding our lives, there is hope for a meaningful journey and a joyous destination.

Words from *Hymns for the Young*
Attributed to DOROTHY A. THRUPP
Music by WILLIAM B. BRADBURY
Arranged by Phillip Keveren

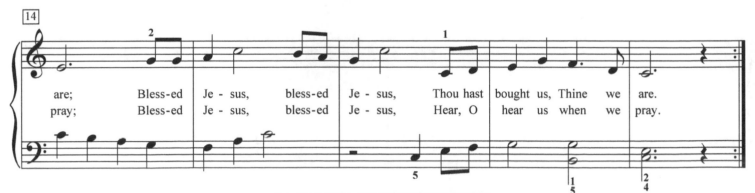

SILENT NIGHT

At the Church of St. Nicholas in Austria, it would have been a strangely silent night at the Christmas Eve Mass had not Joseph Mohr written this hymn text. As assistant priest, Father Joseph was anticipating the beautifully planned musical program for that evening's celebration. However, upon finding the church organ broken, Joseph quickly wrote some lyrics that could be sung without it. He showed the words to the organist, Franz Gruber, who composed a simple tune. That Christmas Eve night in 1818, "Silent Night, Holy Night," was sung with guitar accompaniment. It did not take long for the hymn to spread all over the world, an English translation finally appearing in 1863. It is perhaps the most cherished Christmas hymn of all time.

Words by JOSEPH MOHR
Translated by JOHN F. YOUNG
Music by FRANZ X. GRUBER
Arranged by Phillip Keveren

SOFTLY AND TENDERLY

Will Thompson's secular musical compositions and his publishing company had made him a millionaire. While sitting at a Dwight L. Moody evangelistic meeting, he decided to spend the rest of his days writing Christian music, as a way of giving glory to God for his successes. Shortly after this, in 1880, he wrote the lyrics and tune for "Softly and Tenderly." It became a popular invitational hymn for altar calls at revival services, including those led by Moody. Thompson himself would often load his piano on a horse-drawn wagon and sing his hymns to the poor who could not afford to travel to large Christian conferences. He was humble in spite of his many accomplishments, knowing that Jesus calls all people equally.

Words and Music by
WILL L. THOMPSON
Arranged by Phillip Keveren

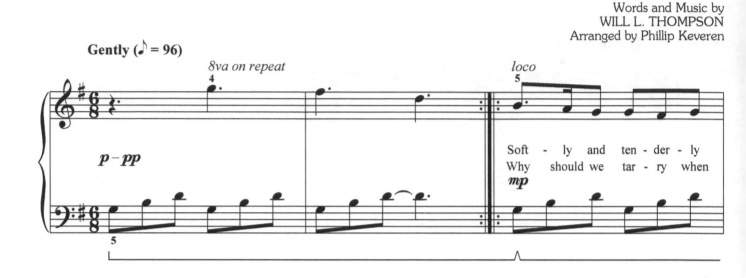

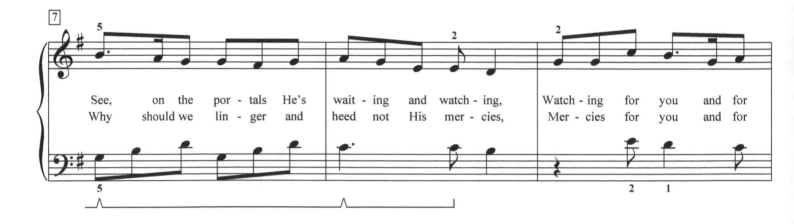

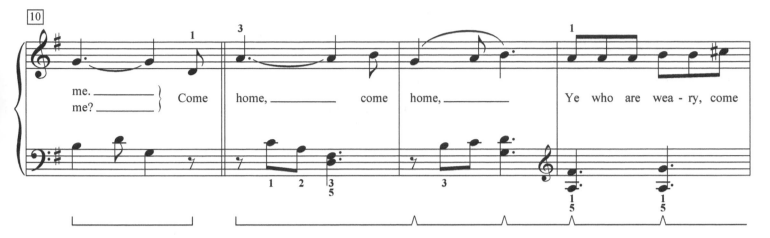

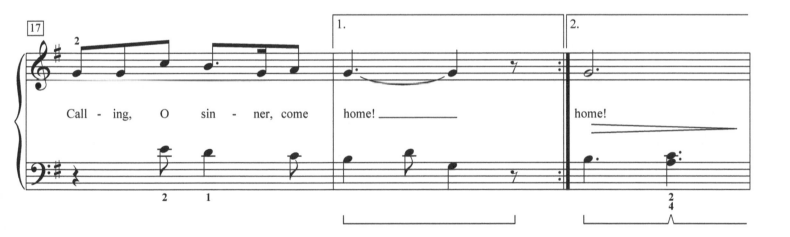

TAKE MY LIFE
AND LET IT BE CONSECRATED

The daughter of a minister, Frances Havergal had confessed Christ for a long time. However, in 1873 at the age of 36, she had an experience where she felt led to give herself more fully to the Lord. Not long after this, she had the opportunity to lead ten people into a fully surrendered devotion to Jesus Christ. One night after this glorious miracle, she struggled to sleep and stayed up writing the lyrics to "Take My Life and Let It Be Consecrated." The words eloquently express what it means to be fully God's. He wants our lives, hands, feet, voice, lips, possessions, and love to be totally given over to Kingdom purposes. When Jesus fills all, there is "full blessedness" (Havergal).

Words by FRANCES R. HAVERGAL
Music by HENRY A. CESAR MALAN
Arranged by Phillip Keveren

At the im - pulse ___ of Thy love.

Take my feet ___ and ___ let them be Swift and beau - ti -

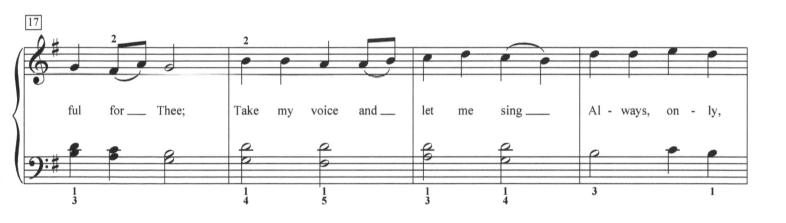

ful for ___ Thee; Take my voice and ___ let me sing ___ Al - ways, on - ly,

for ___ my ___ King, ___ Al - ways, on - ly, ___ for my King.

THERE IS A FOUNTAIN

After losing his mother at the age of six, William Cowper struggled with depression on and off for the rest of his life. At one point, while he and John Newton (who wrote "Amazing Grace") were compiling a book of hymns, he suffered an especially intense bout of depression. In this trial, Cowper meditated upon the power of Christ's blood to save, and he wrote the graphic and deeply emotional lyrics for "There Is a Fountain." In the midst of his emotional struggles, Cowper flung himself totally upon Christ, knowing that Jesus' suffering on his behalf was powerful enough to eventually heal his own deep pain. This hymn is an invitation for all people who suffer to do the same.

Words by WILLIAM COWPER
Traditional American Melody
Arranged by Phillip Keveren

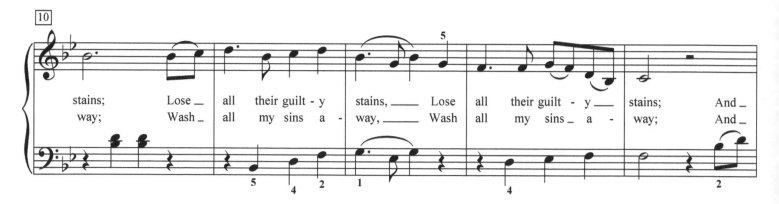

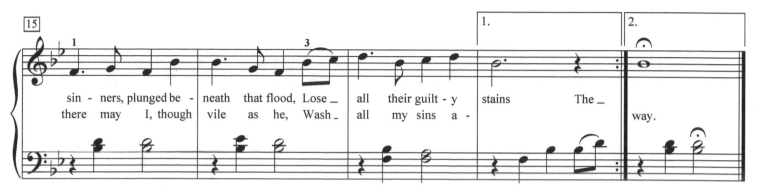

WE GATHER TOGETHER

After decades of political and religious oppression, Holland finally declared its independence from Spain in 1581. A decade later, this hymn text was written by an anonymous Dutchman who, while reflecting on Holland's difficult past, was thankful to his delivering God who "forgets not His own." This hymn is often sung near the Thanksgiving holiday, but it is certainly appropriate for use in giving thanks for God's provision and protection all throughout the year. Especially after God brings His people safely through distressing times, "We Gather Together" helps them declare in unison, "Thou, Lord, wast at our side; all glory be Thine!"

Words from *Nederlandtsch Gedenckclanck*
Translated by THEODORE BAKER
Netherlands Folk Melody
Arranged by Phillip Keveren

'TIS SO SWEET TO TRUST IN JESUS

Around 1880, When Louisa Stead lost her young husband in a freak drowning off the coast of Long Island, she and her four-year-old daughter were devastated. However, Louisa had long-cherished dreams of being a missionary, so she traveled to South Africa to serve God despite their loss. Shortly thereafter, Louisa wrote the lyrics to "'Tis So Sweet to Trust in Jesus." Years later, she was talking about the trials that often await those who love and serve God. She said, "One cannot in the face of the peculiar difficulties help saying, 'Who is sufficient for these things?' but with simple confidence and trust we may and do say, 'Our sufficiency is in God.'" When life is bitter, Jesus is as sweet as ever.

Words by LOUISA M.R. STEAD
Music by WILLIAM J. KIRKPATRICK
Arranged by Phillip Keveren

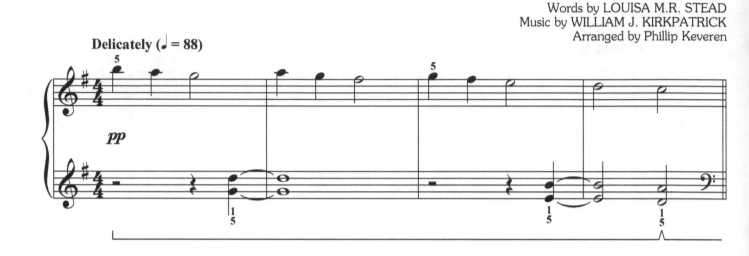

'Tis so sweet to trust in Je - sus, Just to take Him
'Tis so sweet to trust in Je - sus, Just to trust His

at His word; Just to rest up - on His prom - ise,
cleans - ing blood; Just in sim - ple faith to plunge me

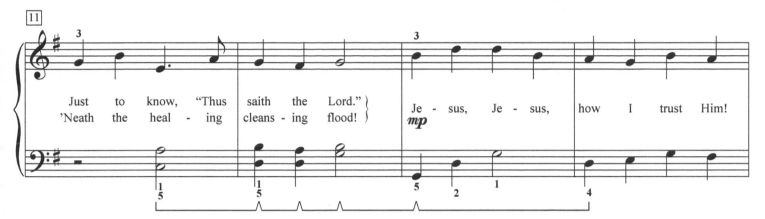

Just to know, "Thus saith the Lord."
'Neath the heal - ing cleans - ing flood! Je - sus, Je - sus, how I trust Him!

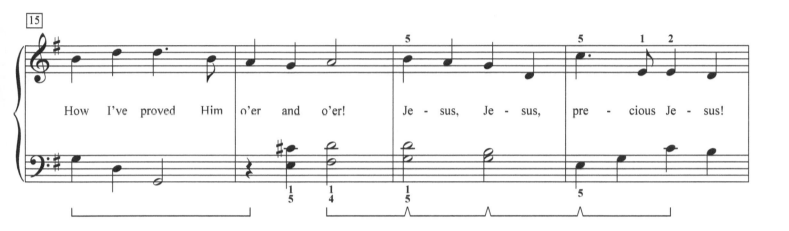

How I've proved Him o'er and o'er! Je - sus, Je - sus, pre - cious Je - sus!

O for grace to trust Him more! trust Him more!

rit.

WERE YOU THERE?

Who better to write this hymn than 19th-century African-American slaves? Who could have possibly identified with Christ's passion better than those who were suffering unthinkable oppression? Who could have better felt the exceeding joy of Christ's victorious resurrection than those who spent their every waking hour longing for freedom from their chains? In Christ's death, all sin and oppression receives its death sentence. In His resurrection, eternal life and deliverance is promised to whosoever calls on Christ as Savior (Jn. 3:16). The slaves who wrote this African-American spiritual were not physically present at Christ's crucifixion or resurrection, but their burdens died with Jesus and their future hopes rose with Him.

Traditional Spiritual
Arranged by Phillip Keveren

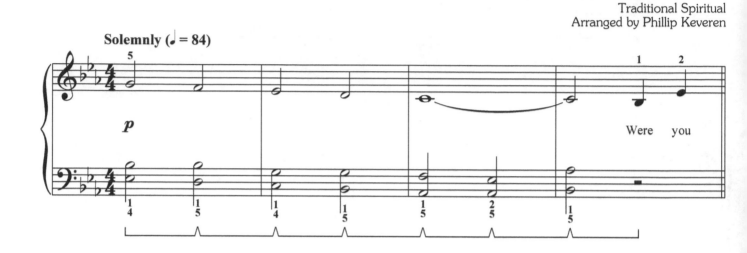

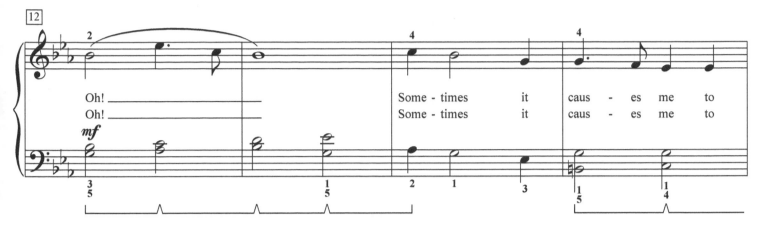

Oh! _____
Oh! _____

Some - times it caus - es me to
Some - times it caus - es me to

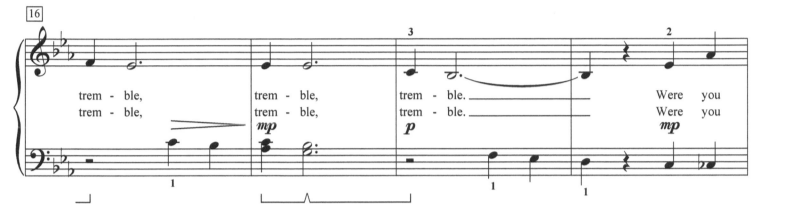

trem - ble,   trem - ble,   trem - ble. _____   Were you
trem - ble,   trem - ble,   trem - ble. _____   Were you

there   when   they   cru - ci - fied   my   Lord? _____
there   when   they   nailed   him   to   the

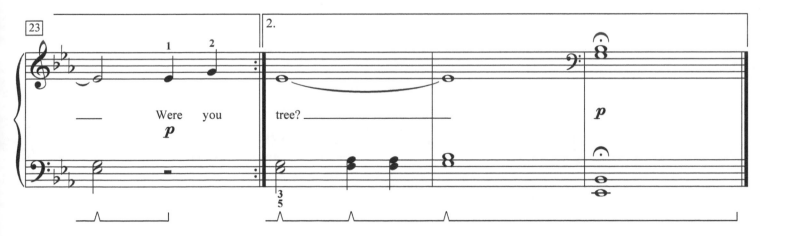

_____ Were   you   tree? _____

WHAT A FRIEND WE HAVE IN JESUS

Joseph Scriven knew what it meant to need the close friendship of Jesus. He had been engaged two times, once in his home country of Ireland and once in Canada, but in both instances, the woman died before the wedding could occur. After these and other misfortunes, Joseph chose to spend his life serving and ministering to suffering people. He spent his time helping the poor, outcasts, widows, and mentally tormented. At one point, his mother became physically ill. Because he could not afford to come to her in Ireland, he wrote and mailed the lyrics of this hymn to comfort her. When later asked to confirm his authorship of the words, as it was published anonymously, he replied "The Lord and I did it between us."

Words by JOSEPH M. SCRIVEN
Music by CHARLES C. CONVERSE
Arranged by Phillip Keveren

WHEN I SURVEY THE WONDROUS CROSS

Isaac Watts is known as the "Father of Modern Hymnody" because his poems helped transition the church of 18th-century England from singing only the psalms in public worship to creatively singing New Testament images and themes. The particular circumstances surrounding Watts's writing of this hymn's lyrics are unknown, but the words are a powerful testimony to the centerpiece of New Testament theology and of a Christian's life. Without the cross of Christ, there is no forgiveness of sin. Had Christ not died, there is no promise of eternal life. Without amazing Love, there is no amazing grace. Love so amazing demands our souls, our lives, our all.

Words by ISAAC WATTS
Music by LOWELL MASON
Arranged by Phillip Keveren

THE PHILLIP KEVEREN SERIES

PIANO SOLO

00156644	**ABBA for Classical Piano**	$15.99
00311024	**Above All**	$12.99
00311348	**Americana**	$12.99
00198473	**Bach Meets Jazz**	$14.99
00313594	**Bacharach and David**	$15.99
00306412	**The Beatles**	$19.99
00312189	**The Beatles for Classical Piano**	$17.99
00275876	**The Beatles – Recital Suites**	$19.99
00312546	**Best Piano Solos**	$15.99
00156601	**Blessings**	$14.99
00198656	**Blues Classics**	$14.99
00284359	**Broadway Songs with a Classical Flair**	$14.99
00310669	**Broadway's Best**	$16.99
00312106	**Canzone Italiana**	$12.99
00280848	**Carpenters**	$17.99
00310629	**A Celtic Christmas**	$14.99
00310549	**The Celtic Collection**	$14.99
00280571	**Celtic Songs with a Classical Flair**	$12.99
00263362	**Charlie Brown Favorites**	$14.99
00312190	**Christmas at the Movies**	$15.99
00294754	**Christmas Carols with a Classical Flair**	$12.99
00311414	**Christmas Medleys**	$14.99
00236669	**Christmas Praise Hymns**	$12.99
00233788	**Christmas Songs for Classical Piano**	$14.99
00311769	**Christmas Worship Medleys**	$14.99
00310607	**Cinema Classics**	$15.99
00301857	**Circles**	$10.99
00311101	**Classic Wedding Songs**	$12.99
00311292	**Classical Folk**	$10.95
00311083	**Classical Jazz**	$14.99
00137779	**Coldplay for Classical Piano**	$16.99
00311103	**Contemporary Wedding Songs**	$12.99
00348788	**Country Songs with a Classical Flair**	$14.99
00249097	**Disney Recital Suites**	$17.99
00311754	**Disney Songs for Classical Piano**	$17.99
00241379	**Disney Songs for Ragtime Piano**	$17.99
00364812	**The Essential Hymn Anthology**	$34.99
00311881	**Favorite Wedding Songs**	$14.99
00315974	**Fiddlin' at the Piano**	$12.99
00311811	**The Film Score Collection**	$15.99
00269408	**Folksongs with a Classical Flair**	$12.99
00144353	**The Gershwin Collection**	$14.99
00233789	**Golden Scores**	$14.99
00144351	**Gospel Greats**	$14.99
00183566	**The Great American Songbook**	$14.99
00312084	**The Great Melodies**	$14.99
00311157	**Great Standards**	$14.99
00171621	**A Grown-Up Christmas List**	$14.99
00311071	**The Hymn Collection**	$14.99
00311349	**Hymn Medleys**	$14.99
00280705	**Hymns in a Celtic Style**	$14.99
00269407	**Hymns with a Classical Flair**	$14.99
00311249	**Hymns with a Touch of Jazz**	$14.99
00310905	**I Could Sing of Your Love Forever**	$16.99
00310762	**Jingle Jazz**	$15.99
00175310	**Billy Joel for Classical Piano**	$16.99
00126449	**Elton John for Classical Piano**	$19.99
00310839	**Let Freedom Ring!**	$12.99
00238988	**Andrew Lloyd Webber Piano Songbook**	$14.99
00313227	**Andrew Lloyd Webber Solos**	$17.99
00313523	**Mancini Magic**	$16.99
00312113	**More Disney Songs for Classical Piano**	$16.99
00311295	**Motown Hits**	$14.99
00300640	**Piano Calm**	$12.99
00339131	**Piano Calm: Christmas**	$14.99
00346009	**Piano Calm: Prayer**	$14.99
00306870	**Piazzolla Tangos**	$17.99
00386709	**Praise and Worship for Classical Piano**	$14.99
00156645	**Queen for Classical Piano**	$17.99
00310755	**Richard Rodgers Classics**	$17.99
00289545	**Scottish Songs**	$12.99
00119403	**The Sound of Music**	$16.99
00311978	**The Spirituals Collection**	$12.99
00366023	**So Far...**	$14.99
00210445	**Star Wars**	$16.99
00224738	**Symphonic Hymns for Piano**	$14.99
00366022	**Three-Minute Encores**	$16.99
00279673	**Tin Pan Alley**	$12.99
00312112	**Treasured Hymns for Classical Piano**	$15.99
00144926	**The Twelve Keys of Christmas**	$14.99
00278486	**The Who for Classical Piano**	$16.99
00294036	**Worship with a Touch of Jazz**	$14.99
00311911	**Yuletide Jazz**	$19.99

EASY PIANO

00210401	**Adele for Easy Classical Piano**	$17.99
00310610	**African-American Spirituals**	$12.99
00218244	**The Beatles for Easy Classical Piano**	$14.99
00218387	**Catchy Songs for Piano**	$12.99
00310973	**Celtic Dreams**	$12.99
00233686	**Christmas Carols for Easy Classical Piano**	$14.99
00311126	**Christmas Pops**	$16.99
00368199	**Christmas Reflections**	$14.99
00311548	**Classic Pop/Rock Hits**	$14.99
00310769	**A Classical Christmas**	$14.99
00310975	**Classical Movie Themes**	$12.99
00144352	**Disney Songs for Easy Classical Piano**	$14.99
00311093	**Early Rock 'n' Roll**	$14.99
00311997	**Easy Worship Medleys**	$14.99
00289547	**Duke Ellington**	$14.99
00160297	**Folksongs for Easy Classical Piano**	$12.99

00110374	**George Gershwin Classics**	$14.99
00310805	**Gospel Treasures**	$14.99
00306821	**Vince Guaraldi Collection**	$19.99
00160294	**Hymns for Easy Classical Piano**	$14.99
00310798	**Immortal Hymns**	$12.99
00311294	**Jazz Standards**	$12.99
00355474	**Living Hope**	$14.99
00310744	**Love Songs**	$14.99
00233740	**The Most Beautiful Songs for Easy Classical Piano**	$12.99
00220036	**Pop Ballads**	$14.99
00311406	**Pop Gems of the 1950s**	$12.95
00233739	**Pop Standards for Easy Classical Piano**	$12.99
00102887	**A Ragtime Christmas**	$12.99
00311293	**Ragtime Classics**	$14.99
00312028	**Santa Swings**	$14.99
00233688	**Songs from Childhood for Easy Classical Piano**	$12.99
00103258	**Songs of Inspiration**	$14.99
00310840	**Sweet Land of Liberty**	$12.99
00126450	**10,000 Reasons**	$16.99
00310712	**Timeless Praise**	$14.99
00311086	**TV Themes**	$14.99
00310717	**21 Great Classics**	$14.99
00160076	**Waltzes & Polkas for Easy Classical Piano**	$12.99
00145342	**Weekly Worship**	$17.99

BIG-NOTE PIANO

00310838	**Children's Favorite Movie Songs**	$14.99
00346000	**Christmas Movie Magic**	$12.99
00277368	**Classical Favorites**	$12.99
00277370	**Disney Favorites**	$14.99
00310888	**Joy to the World**	$12.99
00310908	**The Nutcracker**	$12.99
00277371	**Star Wars**	$16.99

BEGINNING PIANO SOLOS

00311202	**Awesome God**	$14.99
00310837	**Christian Children's Favorites**	$14.99
00311117	**Christmas Traditions**	$10.99
00311250	**Easy Hymns**	$12.99
00102710	**Everlasting God**	$10.99
00311403	**Jazzy Tunes**	$10.95
00310822	**Kids' Favorites**	$12.99
00367778	**A Magical Christmas**	$14.99
00338175	**Silly Songs for Kids**	$9.99

PIANO DUET

00126452	**The Christmas Variations**	$14.99
00362562	**Classic Piano Duets**	$14.99
00311350	**Classical Theme Duets**	$12.99
00295099	**Gospel Duets**	$12.99
00311544	**Hymn Duets**	$14.99
00311203	**Praise & Worship Duets**	$14.99
00294755	**Sacred Christmas Duets**	$14.99
00119405	**Star Wars**	$16.99
00253545	**Worship Songs for Two**	$12.99